A WINTER
IN
MAJORCA

© 1997 Gráficas y Manipulado Mestres, S.A.
Translation of " Un Hiver à Majorque" by George Sand:
Proverb

Printed by Ingrama.sa
Ingrama Editorial, Mallorca, España

D.L.: PM 69- 2002
ISBN 84-85932-37-4

George Sand

A WINTER
IN
MAJORCA

Original title
"Un hiver à Majorque"

AUTHOR'S NOTE

his book can be dated, by glancing at the dedication I wrote to my friend François Rollinat. While the reason I wrote the book, can be found in the reflections that open Chapter Four, which I can only recapitulate here: "Why travel, when you are not obliged to do so?" Today, returning from the same latitude, but from another point in Southern Europe, I can only offer the same justification as I did on returning from Majorca: "The important thing is not to travel, but rather to depart; who among us does not have some pain they wish to escape from, or some bondage they wish to break out of?"

George Sand

Nohant, 25th August 1855

George Sand

(Oil painting by Chapentier. 1839)

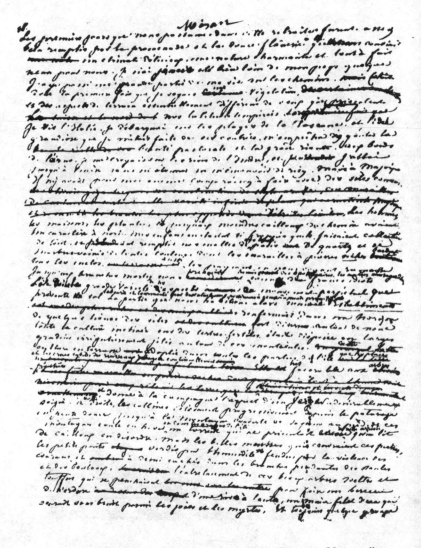

A page from the original manuscript of "A Winter in Majorca"
(Reproduction prohibited). Property of the Frederic Chopin and George Sand Cell, the
Valldemosa Charterhouse.

Frédéric Chopin

(Drawing by Ary Scheffer)

"The Majorcan" (by J. Medinas. J.M. Thomas Collection)

LETTER FROM AN EX- TRAVELLER TO A SEDENTARY FRIEND

y dear Francis, condemned, as you are by duty, to staying at home, you probably think that with my proud, and fickle, independent spirit I would find no greater pleasure in the world than crossing mountains, lakes and valleys. Sadly, my most splendid journeys have been undertaken huddled up next to the fire, with my feet in hot cinders, and my elbows resting on the threadbare sides of my grandmother's armchair. I am sure that you, too, have had such wonderful, and far more poetic, moments. That is why I must tell you that it is a waste of time and effort to regret not having really

sweated in the tropics, or had your feet frozen on the snowy wastes around the pole, or braved horrendous storms at sea, suffered attacks by bandits, or experienced, first hand, any of the dangers, or hazards that you have affronted in your imagination every evening, without ever having kicked off your slippers, and with no other inconvenience than the odd cigar burn along the lining of your smoking jacket.

In order to help reconcile you to your enforced abstinence from physically undertaking such expeditions, I am sending you this description of my latest journey out of France. I am sure that after reading it, you will pity me more than envy me, and that you will feel that I paid too high a price for those brief moments of pleasure in the midst of a run of bad luck.

This description, written a year ago now, has already provoked a powerful, and somewhat comic, diatribe against me by the inhabitants of Majorca. I regret that it is too long to publish as a continuation of my narrative, as the tone in which it was written would only confirm my comments on the hospitality, good taste, and the delicacy which the Majorcans exhibit towards strangers. It would be a peculiar validation to add; but who could possibly read it through to the end? Besides, if it is considered vain and foolish to publish the compliments one has received, would it not be more imprudent, these days, to protest publicly at the injuries to which one is subjected?

I will save you from it then, and restrict myself to commenting, in an attempt to complete the picture I owe you of the ingenuous people of Majorca, that after having read my narrative, the most able lawyers of Palma, (who number forty, I am told), pooling their imaginative efforts, met to compose an indictment of the *immoral writer* who had allowed herself to laugh at their love of profit and their caring concern for the raising of pigs. In this case, one must say, *as did the other one*, that all forty of them had as much wit as four. [1]

As for those good people who were so infuriated by me, let us leave them in peace; they have surely had time to calm down, by now, and I to forget their behaviour, their verbal comments, and what they wrote about me. Indeed, I have largely forgotten the inhabitants of that island now, except for five or six people who, through their hospitality and kindness, will always have a place in my memory, as a compensation and a blessing from Fate. If I do not name them here, it is because I do not consider myself important enough to honour and praise them with my gratitude; I am sure though (and I think I make it clear in the course of my narration), that they will remember me in friendship, and will not believe themselves included in my irreverent jibes, nor doubt my genuine feelings towards them.

I have barely mentioned Barcelona, where we spent a few hectic days before embarking for Majorca. Sailing from Port-Vendres to Barcelona on a good steamer, in

---

[1] This paraphrases a line from Alexis Piron, (1689- 1773) the playwright, another author considered immoral in his time. Sand appears to be punning on the name Quadrado, the author of the diatribe she mentions. The name sounds like *cuadrado* – meaning square, or four sided. (Tr. Note)

fine weather, makes an enchanting cruise. We re-encountered on the Catalan coast, the spring air, that in November we had recently breathed at Nimes, but which had abandoned us in Perpignan; summer heat awaiting us in Majorca. In Barcelona, a fresh sea-breeze tempered the brilliant sunshine, and drove away any sign of cloud from the vast horizon, framed by distant mountain peaks, bare and black, or else white with snow. We took a single trip out into the countryside; but not without ensuring first that the stalwart little Andalusian horses that bore us had eaten all the oats they could eat, in case they had to return us quickly to the safety of the city walls, had we encountered any misadventure.

As you know, at the time of our visit in 1838, there were factious bands of armed malcontents roaming the countryside, setting up road blocks, invading towns and villages, holding to ransom even the smallest private homes, occupying manors as close as half a league from the city, and leaping out from behind nearly every rock to demand of the traveller his purse or his life.

We risked a trip a few leagues up the coast, and met nothing untoward, except for a few detachments of *Christinos*[2] heading towards Barcelona. We were told that they were the best troops in Spain; and it was true that they looked fine, and surprisingly well dressed for men who were in the middle of an active campaign. However, both soldiers and horses were very thin, the former having

---

[2] These would have been troops supporting Maria Christina, the Queen Regent. The opposing forces, supporting a rival bid for the throne by Don Carlos, brother of Fernando VII, were known as Carlists. (Tr. Note)

haggard and jaundiced faces, while the latter hung their heads so low, and had such bony flanks, that to look at them was to be reminded of the pains of hunger.

An even sadder sight was the fortifications that had been raised around the smallest hamlet, and around the door of even the tiniest shack. These normally consisted of a dry-stone wall, topped by a crenellated tower, whose walls were no more solid than nougat, in front of every gate; or else small walls, with embrasures around each roof, testament to the fact that no inhabitant of this fertile area believed himself safe. In many places, the ruins of these modest fortifications showed signs of having recently been attacked, or defended.

However, once we entered the formidable and immense fortifications around Barcelona, passing through countless gates, drawbridges, portcullis and ramparts, there was little to substantiate the fact that the city was at war. Behind a triple ring of cannon, isolated from the rest of Spain by banditry and civil war, the radiant youth of Barcelona strolled up and down the *Rambles*, that long avenue of trees and houses, similar to a French boulevard: the women beautiful, graceful and coquettish, preoccupied only with the fold of their mantillas, and the play of their fans; the men, concerned with their cigars, laughing, chatting, looking at the ladies out of the corner of their eyes, entertaining themselves with Italian opera, and with no outward show that they were the least worried about what was happening on the other side of the walls. However, when night fell, the opera had finished, and the guitars had been packed away, the city was handed over to the *serenos*[3] on their beat, and the only sounds one could hear above the monotonous surging of the sea were the menacing cries of the sentries, and the even more ominous sound of shots, sometimes heard separately, sometimes simultaneously, and from different points, sometimes at a distance, other times much closer to hand, and always continuing until the first light of the dawn. Then, all would remain peaceful for an hour or two, and it seemed that the Bourgeoisie slept profoundly, while the port awoke, and the sailors began to go about their daily business.

If, during the daylight hours of strolling and gossiping, you should ask anyone what those strange, alarming noises you had heard during the night were, they would smile, and reply that nobody took any notice of them, and it were better not to enquire after them.

---

3 Night watchmen. (Tr. Note)

FIRST PART

CHAPTER ONE

ome fifty years ago, I believe, two English tourists discovered the Alpine valley of Chamonix, or at least that is what the inscription they left chiselled onto a rock at the entrance to the *Mer-de-Glace* glacier claims.

Such an assertion may seem a trifle exaggerated if we consider the geographical position of this petite valley, but legitimate, up to a point, if those tourists, whose names I have forgotten, were the first to introduce these romantic sites to the poets and painters or to Byron, who dreamed up his admirable drama *Manfred* there.

One could say, in fact, that Switzerland had not really

been discovered by fashionable society or by the artistic community until the last century. Jean-Jacques Rousseau is the true Christopher Columbus of Alpine poetry, and, as Monsieur de Chateaubriand rightly remarked, also the father of romanticism in the French language.

Not having precisely the same entitlement to immortality as Jean-Jacques, and reflecting upon those assets I could be said to have, I find that I might perhaps have followed the example of the two Englishmen at Chamonix and claimed the honour of having discovered the isle of Majorca. However, the world has become such an exacting place that it would not be enough nowadays for me to merely carve my name on a Balearic rock. The world would now demand that I write an exact description, or at least a sufficiently poetic narrative, of my journey, which would prompt the people who read it to wish to emulate my travels. Having not exactly felt ecstatic during my sojourn in that country, I renounce the glory of my discovery and make no such claim, either in stone or on paper.

If I had written under the influence of the inconveniences and frustrations that I experienced then, it would not have been possible for me to have spoken highly of my discovery, since anyone reading the work would have told me that I had little right to make any lofty claims for it. However, I do think I can be bold enough to declare today that Majorca, for painters, is one of the most beautiful countries on Earth, and one of the least publicized. There, where there is nothing else to describe but picturesque beauty, literary attempts to express it look so meagre and so inadequate that I have barely attempted it. It would take an artist's pencil or an engraver's burin to communicate, to the travel enthusiast, the grandeur and charm of nature there.

If, today, I have chosen to shake the lethargic dust off my memories of that time, it is because one morning, recently, I found upon my table a delightful volume entitled *Memories of an Artist's Voyage to the Isle of Majorca*, by J.B. Laurens.

It was a veritable joy for me to rediscover Majorca, with its palm trees, its aloes, the vestiges of its Moorish past and its Greek attire. I recognised all of the poetic colour of the sites illustrated and revived all of my already forgotten, or at least I had believed them forgotten, impressions. There was not a hovel or a bramble hedge that did not call up in me a whole world of memories, as we say today. It was then that I felt myself strong enough, if not to describe my journey, then at least to review that of M. Laurens, an intelligent and painstaking artist, who works swiftly and conscientiously. The honour of discovering the island of Majorca, which I have relinquished, should undoubtedly be bestowed upon him.

M. Laurens' journey into the heart of the Mediterranean, along shores where the sea is sometimes as inhospitable as the inhabitants, is so much more worthy of praise than the excursion of our two

23

Englishmen to Montanvert. Nevertheless, if European civilisation ever reaches the point at which it eradicates customs barriers and policemen, those visible manifestations of distrust and national antipathies; if steamships are ever organised directly from France to these vicinities, then Majorca will be a powerful rival for Switzerland; since once it is possible to travel there in as few days, people will no doubt discover there beauties as mellow, and grandeurs as strange and sublime. All of which will provide new sustenance for painting.

However, at the present time, in all conscience, I could only recommend this voyage to artists who are physically robust and passionate of spirit. No doubt a time will come when the delicate amateur, or even attractive ladies, will be able to visit Palma without any more trouble or effort than they would experience in visiting Geneva.

M. Laurens has long been associated with the endeavours of M. Taylor with regards the ancient monuments of France. Last year, left to his own devices, M. Laurens decided to visit the Balearics. He knew so little about the islands that he confesses to have felt his heart beat wildly as he stepped ashore onto a land where perhaps so many disappointments might await him as a reaction to his optimistic dreams. However, it would be difficult for him not to find what he was searching for there, and all his dreams probably came true; since, I repeat, Majorca is an El Dorado for painters. Everything there is picturesque, from the peasant's hut, which has preserved something of a Moorish influence, even in the lowliest construction, to the child dressed in tatters, triumphant in his *grandiose grubbiness*, to appropriate a phrase Heinrich Heine used to describe the women of the herb market in Verona. The character of the landscape, generally richer in vegetation than that of North Africa, demonstrates the same breadth, calm and simplicity. There is Helvetian green, under a Calabrian sky, amidst the solemnity and silence of the Orient.

In Switzerland, the relentlessly roaring waters and the constantly passing clouds give the views a mobility of colour, or to put it another way, a continuity of movement that painting does not always manage to successfully reproduce. Nature there appears to mock the artist, while in Majorca, it appears to wait upon or invite the artist. The vegetation takes on shapes that are arrogant and bizarre, but without displaying that untidy luxury into which the lines of the Swiss landscape too often disappear. The peaks of the crags define their immobile contours against a dazzling sky, the palm trees lean over precipices without letting the capricious breezes disturb the majesty of their mane of fronds, and even the most stunted cactus at the side of the path seems to pose, like everything else, in a kind of vanity designed to please the eye.

Before adding anything else, I will go on to give a very concise description of the Balearic Major, of a type commonly found in an article in a geographical primer. This is not as easy a task as one might expect, above all when one is seeking such information in the country itself. The prudence of the Spaniard and the mistrust of the islander are so exaggerated that a stranger cannot address even the idlest question to anyone, without the risk of being taken for a spy. The good M. Laurens was actually imprisoned, by the mistrustful governor, for the crime of having made a sketch of a castle in ruins that had taken his fancy. He was accused of drawing up plans of fortifications[1]. After that, our traveller decided to fill his sketch book anywhere but in the prisons of the State of Majorca. Subsequently, he made sure that he confined his questions to the whereabouts of the paths into the mountains and that he did not consult any other document but the stones of the ruins themselves. After having spent four months on Majorca, I would not have

---

[1] "The only thing that attracted my attention on that shore was some dark-ochre coloured ruins surrounded by a wall of cacti. It was the Castle of Soller. I had barely drawn the basic outlines of my sketch when I saw four individuals fast approaching. They were rather frightening, if a little comical, in appearance. They told me that I was guilty of breaking the laws of the realm by having drawn up plans of a fortress; a fortress that was soon to become my prison.

"I was far from eloquent enough in Spanish to try to convince them of the absurdity of their accusation; hence I had to resort to the protection of the French consul in Soller. Despite his efforts on my behalf, I was still held captive for three mortal hours, guarded by Señor *Sei-Dedos*, [Six Fingers] the governor of the fort, a veritable dragon of the Hesperides. I was often tempted to throw that preposterous dragon, and his military accoutrement, from the heights of his bastion into the sea; but his appearance always undermined my rage. If I had possessed the talent of Charlet, I would have passed my time studying my governor as an excellent model for a caricature. In the end, I forgave his blind devotion to the health of the state. It was only natural that this poor man, who had no other distraction than to smoke his cigar gazing out to sea, would seize the opportunity I offered him to vary his routine. I returned, then to Soller, heartily laughing at having been taken for an enemy of the fatherland and the constitution." (*Memories of an Artistic Voyage to the Isle of Majorca*, by J.B. Laurens.) [Author's Note]

got any further than he, had I not consulted what little information was available on the region. However this is where my doubts began to creep in again; because these already out-of-date works often contradict one another. Following the tradition of traveller's tales, they haughtily denigrate the accounts of others and accuse them of falsehoods in such a way that one is left with the desire to rectify some of the misrepresentations at the risk of committing many more. Here then is my entry for a geographical primer; and so as not to stray from my role as a genuine traveller I will begin by declaring them to be undeniably superior to all those that have gone before.

CHAPTER TWO

ajorca, which Mr Laurens, like the Romans, calls *Balearis Major*, and which the king of Majorcan historians, Dr Juan Dameto, says was once known as *Clumba* or *Columba*, is called today, through corruption, Mallorca. The capital of the island has never been known as Majorca, despite what many of our atlases claim, but rather Palma.

This island is the largest and most fertile of the Balearic archipelago, which is a vestige of a continent whose lowlands the Mediterranean must have submerged and which doubtless once united Spain with Africa; it shares some of the climate and produce of both. It is situated some 25 leagues south-east of Barcelona and 45 from the nearest point on the African coast, and I believe some 95 or a 100 from the harbour of Toulon. It has a surface area of 1,234 square miles with a perimeter of 143. At its widest point it measures 54 miles and at its narrowest 28. Its population, which in 1787 comprised 136,000 individuals, is today around 160,000. The town of Palma has 36,000 residents today, as opposed to 32,000 at that time.

The temperature varies notably, depending on the diverse orientations of the island. Summers are scorching throughout the plain, but the chain of mountains that extends from the north-east to the south west (an angle which reinforces the island's identity with the territories of Africa and Spain, whose closest points are also oriented thus) greatly influences the winter temperatures. Miguel de Vargas reports that in the bay of Palma, during the terrible winter of 1784, the temperature only dropped to 6 degrees, on the Reaumur scale, once, on a single day in January. On other days it rose to 16, but it was usually around 11 degrees. This latter figure being more or less what we ourselves experienced for the most part during an ordinary winter in the mountains around Valldemosa, which has the reputation of being one of the coldest places on the island. On the harshest nights, when we had about two inches of snow, the thermometer hovered around 6 or 7 degrees. At eight o'clock in the morning it had risen to 9 or 10 and by midday was up to 12 or 14. Ordinarily, around three o'clock, which is to say after the sun had gone down, for us, behind the surrounding mountain peaks, the temperature fell suddenly to 9 and even 8 degrees.

The northern winds often blow there with a fury, and, some years, the winter rains come down with an abundance and continuousness that we in France can barely imagine. In general, the climate is healthy and generous throughout the meridional region, which descends towards Africa, and which is protected from the severe squalls of the north by the range of hills that crosses the middle of the island, and by the considerable escarpment running along the northern coast. So, in general, the island has a surface that slopes from north-west to south-east and navigation, almost impossible in the north due to the chasms and cliffs along a coast that is *escarpada y horrorosa, sin abrigo ni resguardo*[1] (Miguel de Vargas), although safe and sure in the south.

* * *

Despite its wild winds and its ruggedness, Majorca, was rightly named by the ancients, the "golden isle". It is extremely fertile and its products are of an exquisite quality. The wheat flour there is so pure and good that the inhabitants export it to Barcelona where it is used to make light, white pastries, known as *pan de Mallorca*.

---

[1] In Spanish in the original text: "...precipitous, horrendous, with neither shelter nor protection from the elements" (Tr. Note)

The Majorcans import cheaper and lower grade flour from Galicia and Biscay from which they make their own bread. In other words, in a country rich in excellent wheat, people eat bread that is simply detestable. I have no idea if this speculation is really advantageous for them.

In our central provinces, where agriculture is behind the times, the usual attitude of our peasants only serves to prove their obstinacy and ignorance. This is even truer in Majorca where agriculture, despite being meticulously tended, appears to still be in its infancy. Nowhere else have I seen the land worked so patiently, yet with such inefficiency. Even the simplest agricultural machinery is unknown on the island; human arms much thinner and weaker than ours, handle everything, although with a singular sluggishness. It takes them half a day to dig less ground than our farmers would turn over in two hours, and it needs five or six of the most robust men to lift a load that the weakest of our porters would swing up cheerily onto his shoulders.

Despite this apparent lack of concern, everywhere is cultivated, and apparently well cultivated, in Majorca. The islanders claim not to be familiar with deprivation; but amidst the best of nature's treasures, and beneath the most beautiful of skies, their lives are more rudimentary and more dolefully dull than that of our own peasants.

Travellers are wont to make statements about the contentment of the peoples of the south. They see them on Sundays with their picturesque costumes, and faces lit by the rays of the sun, and they take their lack of ideas and expectations to be an example of the ideal serenity of country life. It is an error that I myself have even committed, though one I will never repeat, especially after having seen Majorca.

There is nothing sadder or poorer in the world than the peasant who only knows how to pray, sing, work, and who never thinks. Their prayer is a meaningless formula which offers nothing to their spirit; their work is an exertion of muscles that no effort of their intelligence has taught them to simplify; and their song is an expression of that dismal melancholy that overwhelms them without their even being aware of it, and which has a poetic effect on us that is hidden from them. If it were not for the vanity that from time to time rouses them from their torpor to get them up to dance, their local holidays would be entirely devoted to sleep.

However, I digress from the framework I have set myself. I had forgotten that in the strict guidelines laid down by tradition, the geographical article must mention, above all, the productive and commercial economy and must only refer to the human species as a last resort, after having dealt with cereals and cattle.

In all the geographical articles I have consulted on the Balearics, I have always found the following assertion, which I confirm here, though reserving the right to comment later on its validity: "The islanders are *very friendly* (as is well known, on every island, the human race can be divided into two categories, those that are cannibals and those that are very friendly). They are kind, hospitable; they very rarely commit crimes and theft is almost unheard of there". I will disclose the truth behind these assertions presently.

Beforehand, we must talk about produce, as I believe certain remarks (imprudent, at least) have been spoken in Parliament about a possible occupation of Majorca by the French, and I presume that if this text were to fall into the hands of one of our Members of Parliament, he would be more interested in the parts dealing with merchandise, than with my philosophic deliberations on the intellectual prowess of the Majorcans.

* * *

I can affirm then, that the soil of Majorca is of an admirable fertility and that a more active and wiser cultivation of it would multiply production. The principal export consists of almonds, oranges and pigs. Oh, beautiful trees of the Hesperides, guarded by those filthy dragons, it is not my fault if I am forced to remember you along with those ignoble swine of which the Majorcans are more jealous and proud than of your fragrant flowers and your golden apples! Sadly, the Majorcan who tends you is no more poetic than the Member of Parliament who reads me.

Let me return to my pigs. These animals, dear reader, are the most beautiful on earth, and Dr. Miguel Vargas, with the most naïve admiration, has portrayed a young

34

hog which, at the tender age of a year and a half, weighs twenty-four *arrobas*, that is to say six hundred pounds. In those days, the husbandry of pigs in Majorca had not attained the splendour that it has in our time. The trade in animals was hindered by the rapacity of the Majorcan suppliers, in whom the Spanish government had put their trust, that is to say to whom they had sold the entitlement to provide provisions. As a result of their discretionary powers, these Majorcan speculators opposed all export of livestock, and reserved for themselves the right to unlimited importation.

The result of this avaricious practice was that it deterred the locals from taking proper care of their herds. Meat was being sold at a ludicrously low price and, as exports were banned, growers had little choice but to accept their ruin or to abandon husbandry altogether. Extinction occurred promptly. The historian, who I quote, bewailed the fact that in Majorca, at the time of the Moorish occupation, and on the mountain of Arta alone, there were once more head of fertile cows and noble bulls than could now be gathered together across the entire Majorcan plain.

Unfortunately, this was not the only rich natural resource allowed to slide into decrepitude; the same writer reports that the mountains, particularly those at Torella and Galatzo, once possessed the most beautiful trees in the world. There was a certain olive tree that measured forty-two feet in circumference and fourteen in diameter; but those magnificent forests were devastated by naval carpenters, who, in response to the Spanish expedition against Algeria, built an entire fleet of men o'war with them. The vexations to which the owners of these forests were then subjected, and the pittance with which they were compensated, persuaded the Majorcans to destroy their forests rather than enlarge them. Today, the vegetation is still so abundant and beautiful that the traveller need not yearn for the past; but today, as then, in Majorca, as in the whole of Spain, the abuse of power is still the primary use of power. However, the traveller will not hear a single complaint, because at the beginning of an unjust regime, the powerless hold their tongues out of fear, and when the evil is established, they keep mum out of habit.

Even though the tyranny of the Majorcan suppliers has disappeared, husbandry has still not recovered from its ruin, nor will it, while the right to export is limited to trading in pigs. One sees very few heads of beef or cows across the plain, and none in the mountains. Meat is lean and tough. The sheep are of good stock, but they are poorly fed and badly looked after. The goats, which are of African stock, do not give even a tenth of the milk that ours do.

The soil needs manure and, despite the eulogies the Majorcans deliver about their methods of cultivation, I believe that the seaweed they use for the purpose is a very poor substitute, and that the land produces far less than it should produce under that generous sky. I have looked carefully at that precious wheat that the inhabitants do not believe themselves worthy enough to eat: it is exactly the same as that which we grow in our central provinces, and which our peasants call white wheat or Spanish wheat; it is equally fine in our fields, despite the difference in climate. However, the wheat of Majorca should be markedly superior to that which we struggle to produce, given our harsh winters and unpredictable springs. Yet our agriculture is primitive too, and we have much to learn in the field, but the French peasant has a perseverance and energy that the Majorcan scorns as if it were a disorderly disturbance.

The fig, the olive, the almond and the orange are found in abundance in Majorca; however the lack of roads in the interior of the island mean that their commercialisation is not nearly as extensive or active as it needs to be. Five hundred oranges can be bought at an orange grove for three francs, but to transport such a bulky cargo from the centre to the coast, on the backs of mules, one would need to spend as much again. This consideration leads to the neglect of orange cultivation in the interior of the island. It is only in the Soller valley and around the coves where our small ships are loaded, that these trees grow in abundance. However, they will grow well anywhere. Even on our mountain at Valldemosa, one of the coldest regions on the island, we had magnificent lemons and oranges, though they ripened a little later than those of Soller. At *La Granja*, in another mountainous region, we picked lemons as big as a man's head. I believe that Majorca alone could supply the entire needs of France for this exquisite fruit at the same price as those detestable oranges that we get from Hyres and the Genovese coast. This trade, much praised on Majorca, is, like everything else, currently in a state of terrible negligence.

The same could be said of the enormous production harvested from the olive groves, certainly the most beautiful trees in the world, and which the Majorcans, thanks to Moorish traditions, know how to cultivate perfectly. Sadly, they only seem to know how to produce an olive oil that is rancid and nauseous and which would horrify us.[2] They will never be able to export it in any great quantity to anywhere but Spain, where the taste of this infected oil is to be found everywhere. But Spain itself is rich in olive trees, so if Majorca is supplying it with olive oil, it must be at an extremely low price.

We consume an enormous amount of olive oil in France, and that which we have is of poor quality and sold at an exorbitant price. If they were aware in Majorca of our manufacturing methods, and if Majorca had the roads, and shipping lines, in short, if commerce were well organised in this sphere, we would have olive

---

[2] This oil is so ubiquitous on the island of Majorca that the houses, inhabitants, carriages, even the air from the fields, indeed everything, is impregnated with its stench. As it is used in every meal, cooking fumes laden with it infect every house two or three times a day and the walls are steeped in it. Even out in the country, if you become lost, you only have to open your nostrils and if a whiff of rancid oil wafts towards you on the breeze you can be sure that around the next rock or beneath the next mass of cacti there will be a dwelling. If you catch a hint of that odour in even the most remote and wild part of the island, lift up your head and you will surely perceive, some hundred paces from your position, a Majorcan descending the hill, coming towards you on an ass. This is not a yarn or mere hyperbole, it is the simple truth. (Author's Note).

oil at a much cheaper price than we currently pay, and we would have it pure and abundant, however harsh the winter. I am aware that the industrialists who cultivate the olive of peace in France far prefer to sell a few tons of this precious liquid for its weight in gold, and that our shopkeepers mix it with peanut or rapeseed oil, in order to be able to offer it to us *at cost*; but it would be strange if someone were to insist on struggling with the rigours of the climate in order to produce something which they could obtain, cheaper and superior in quality, a mere twenty-four hours' sail away.

However, our French suppliers need have no fears just yet. If we were to promise the Majorcan, and I feel the Spaniard in general, that we would furnish all our needs from them and multiply their wealth tenfold, they would still not change their ingrained habits. They despise profoundly any improvement that comes from abroad, above all from France, so I do not know if they would change any of the habits they have inherited from their forebears for any amount of money (even though, in general they do not spurn this latter commodity).

CHAPTER THREE

s they do not know how to fatten their oxen, nor utilise wool, nor milk cows (the Majorcans abhor milk and butter as much as they despise toil); without knowing how to produce enough wheat to dare to eat it; without stooping to cultivate mulberries and gather in silk; having lost the art of joinery, once so flourishing and now almost completely forgotten; not having horses (acting maternally, Spain takes possession of all of the colts on Majorca for its army, and the pacific Majorcans are not so simple as to work to provide the cavalry of the realm); not feeling the need for even a single road, a single serviceable path on the entire island, since the

right to export depends on the whim of a government that has not got the time to concern itself with such trivialities, the Majorcans vegetated and had nothing better to do than say the rosary, patch their breeches, more ragged than that of Don Quixote, their patron in misery and pride, when the pig came to save the day. Export of this quadruped was authorized, and a new era, the era of salvation, began.

In centuries to come, the Majorcans will remember this century as the age of the pig, as the Muslims remember in their history the age of the elephant.

Now the ground is no longer carpeted in olives and carob pods, the fruit of the prickly pear is no longer a mere child's toy, and the mothers of the family have learned to economise on beans and potatoes. The pig does not allow the waste of anything, because the pig does not leave anything to be wasted. The animal is the best example of unrestrained voracity, coupled to a simplicity of tastes and manners, which one could hope to show to the world. In fact, the creature enjoys rights and prerogatives in Majorca that until now nobody had thought to offer to the human inhabitants. Dwellings have been enlarged and aired, fruit that used to rot on the ground has been harvested, classified and preserved; and steamships, until recently considered superfluous and irrational, have now been established from the island to the continent.

It is thanks to the pig, then, that I have visited the isle of Majorca, since, had I planned to go there three years

42

ago, the long and hazardous voyage aboard a coastal trader would have made me think twice about going. However, since the exportation of pigs has been allowed, civilisation has begun to penetrate the island.

A small and attractive steamer was bought in England, that is not sufficiently large to fight the terrible gales that the northern waters of the island are prone to, but nonetheless, when the seas are calm, transports two hundred pigs and a few passengers over to Barcelona once a week.

It is pleasing to see how the passengers are treated with such consideration and tenderness on board (and I am not talking about the humans here) and with what loving care they are disembarked onto land again. The captain of the steamer is a very amiable fellow who, having been forced to live among, and talk to, these noble creatures, has taken on something of their diction and casual manners. If a passenger should complain about the noise they make, the captain replies that it is the sound of golden coins rolling across the counter. If a lady is fussy enough to remark on the pestilent stench spreading throughout the ship, her husband is on hand to reply that money smells sweet and that without the pigs there would be no silk dresses for her, nor French millinery, nor mantillas from Barcelona. Should anyone feel sea-sick, they should not attempt to elicit the slightest sympathy from any of the crew, because the pigs also get sea-sick and in them this indisposition is accompanied by a splenetic languor and a loss of the will to live that must be combated at all cost. Thus, abjuring all compassion and sympathy in order to safeguard the existence of their dearest customers, the captain in person, armed with a whip, plunges amongst them, with his sailors and cabin boys behind him, each grabbing whatever comes to hand, one a steel bar, another a length of rope and in a moment the entire group of mute and prone animals is whacked on their sides, in a paternal way, and obliged to get up and move around, this violent emotion thus combating the evil influence of the rolling waves.

When we were returning to Barcelona from Majorca, in the month of March, it was a suffocatingly hot day, but even so it was still not possible to go out on deck. Even if we had been willing to face the danger of having our legs bitten off by some bad tempered pig, the captain would surely have forbidden us from upsetting them with our presence. The animals were calm during the first hours of the voyage, but, in the middle of the night, the pilot remarked that they were in a stupor and appeared to be the victims of a black melancholy. Consequently, the whip was administered; and regularly, every quarter of an hour, we were woken by terrifying cries and shrieks from the hurt and angry pigs on the one hand, and on the other by the shouts of encouragement from the captain and the swearing, that emulation had inspired, of his men. We were frequently concerned that the herd would devour the entire crew.

Once we had dropped anchor, we were, of course, anxious to leave the company of our peculiar companions and I must confess that the company of the islanders was beginning to oppress me quite as much as that of the others. However, we were not permitted to take the air until after the pigs had been disembarked. We could have asphyxiated in our cabins, and nobody would have batted an eyelid while there was yet a single pig to off load and deliver from the rising and falling of the sea.

I have no fear of the deep, but one member of my family was dangerously ill. The crossing, the foul stench, and the lack of sleep had not contributed to diminishing his suffering. The only concern the captain had showed us was to request that we not put our invalid in the best bed in the cabin, because in accordance with Spanish prejudices, every illness was considered contagious, and as the captain planned to burn the bunk on which the sick person had lain, he wished to ensure that we placed him in the worst bunk in the room. We left our host to his pigs, and a fortnight later when we returned to France aboard the *Phoenician*, a magnificent steamship from our nation, we compared the self-sacrifice of the French with the hospitality of the Spanish. The captain of the *Mallorquín* had begrudged a bed to a dying man; the captain from Marseilles considered our invalid not sufficiently comfortable and took off the mattress from his own bed to give to him. When I wished to pay for our passage, the Frenchman told me I was offering him too much, while the Majorcan had made me pay double.

However, I do not conclude from this that people are exclusively good in one part of this *terraqueous globe*, nor exclusively bad in another. Wickedness in humanity is usually the result of material needs. Suffering engenders fear, mistrust, fraud, and struggle in the widest sense of the word. The Spaniard is ignorant and superstitious; consequently he believes in contagion, he fears disease and death, and lacks both faith and charity. He is wretched and is weighed down by taxes; consequently he is grasping, selfish, and cheats foreigners. History shows us that whenever the Spaniard could be great, he was capable of greatness, but he is only human, and in private life, where men can succumb, they will succumb.

I need to establish this as a principle, before going on to talk about my perception of the men of Majorca, because I think I have now discharged my duty towards the olives, cows and pigs. The very length of this last article is not in good taste. I beg the pardon of those who may feel personally wounded, and I now continue my narrative in earnest, because I believed, when I started it, that I would do no more than to follow the footsteps of M. Laurens in his *Artistic Voyage*, but I see now that when my memory returns to the rugged paths of Majorca, I am assailed by a multitude of reflections.

CHAPTER FOUR

ut if you do not understand painting, they would say to me, *what on earth were you doing in that confounded gallery?* I would like to divert the reader with me and mine as little as possible. However, I will be forced to often refer, when speaking about what I saw in Majorca, to *me* and *us*. *I* and *we* represents a fortuitous *subjectivity*, without which certain aspects of the *objectivity* of the Majorcans would not have been revealed, which, perhaps, it would be genuinely useful now to disclose to the reader. I beg of you then to consider my personality as a completely passive element here. Consider me a pair of binoculars through which

one might view what is happening in a distant land, so that one might willingly say, to paraphrase the proverb: I prefer to believe it, rather than to see it for myself. I beseech you also to trust that I have not the least intention of trying to interest you in any accidents that befell me. My aim is a little too philosophical to describe those here, and when I have marshalled my thoughts in this respect, I hope that all will do me the justice of recognising that I do not exhibit the slightest concern for myself in these pages.

I will tell the reader then, without vacillation, why I entered that gallery, and I can sum it up in few words: I yearned to travel. And now I will ask you a question, dear reader: when you travel, why do you travel? I believe I can hear from here what you would reply, it is what I would say in your place:

"I travel to travel".

I know very well that travelling for its own sake is a pleasure; but seriously, what drives you to this extravagant, tiring, and at times, perilous diversion, which is always plagued with countless disappointments?

"The need to travel!"

Ah, fine! But tell me then, what is this necessity? Why are we all more or less obsessed by it, and why do we all give in to it, even after having recognised, time and again, that it has taken us over and will never leave us, and is never satisfied with anything?

If you do not wish to reply, I will take it upon myself to answer for you. The fact is that, in this age, none of

General view of Palma de Mallorca
(Drawing by Parcerisa)

Son Vent (Establiments)
The house Chopin and George Sand inhabited, before moving
into the Valldemosa Charterhouse (drawing by Maurice Sand)

us, anywhere, are really content to be where we are, and because of all the shapes that the *ideal* takes on (if the word displeases you, perhaps the *desire for improvement* will not), travelling is one of the most cheerful, and the most misleading. Officialdom has gone from bad to worse: those who deny it feel as deeply about it as those that affirm it, and they do so even more bitterly. However, divine hope continues to follow its course, carrying out its work on our hearts, and always filling us with this sensation of a potentially better world, this quest for the ideal.

The social order, which fails to even arouse the sympathies of those who support it, satisfies none of us, and each of us goes willy-nilly wherever they please. One plunges into the arts, another into the sciences, the majority merely amuse themselves however they can. Everyone who has a little leisure time, and the money, travels; or perhaps it would be more accurate to say flees, since the important thing is not to travel, but rather to depart, do you follow me? Who among us does not have some pain they wish to escape from, or some bondage they wish to break out of? Nobody!

Anyone who is not absorbed in their work, or numbed by indolence, is incapable, I maintain, of staying for long in one place without suffering, and without desiring a change. If anyone is happy (they would need to be very illustrious or very cowardly to be so today), they still imagine they would feel even better travelling; do not as many lovers and newly weds set off for Switzerland and

Italy as idlers and hypochondriacs? In a few words, anyone who feels alive or disheartened becomes consumed by the zeal of the wandering Jew, and sets off for distant shores in search of the better life, or a love nest, or a place in which to curl up and die.

Heaven forbid that I should proclaim myself against the movement of populations, and imagine a future in which people are tied to a country, a field, or a house, like polyps to a sponge! However, if intelligence and morality are to progress in chorus with industry, it seems to me that the railways should not be destined to carry, from one point of the globe to another, populations inflicted with spleen, or consumed by some unhealthy activity.

I wish to imagine a happier human race, one that is more peaceful and more enlightened, having two lives: one being sedentary, full of domestic bliss, the responsibilities of the city, studious meditation and philosophical musing; the other, active, dedicated to the honourable interchange with which I would replace the shameful traffic that we call commerce, to the inspiration of the arts, to scientific research and, above all, to the propagation of ideas. In short, I believe that the driving force behind our journeys is a lack of contact, of relationship, of sympathetic dealings with other people, and that pleasure in that should not exist without obligation. However, it seems to me, that most of us travel, today, in search of mystery or isolation, and with a distrust of what the company of others might do to our personal impressions, whether they be pleasant or disagreeable.

As for me, I set off on the road to satisfy a need for rest that I feel particularly strongly, in this day and age. As there is no time to do everything in this world we have created, I imagine, once again, that if I look hard enough, I am going to find some quiet, isolated retreat, where I would not have to write cards, or peruse newspapers, nor have to entertain visitors, or take off my dressing gown; where the days would be twelve hours long, where I could be free of all social conventions, disconnected from the intellectual movement that is consuming the whole of France, and where I would be able to dedicate a year or two to the study of history and also to learning my language *from first principles*, with my children.

Who among us has never had a similar selfish dream, of one day just abandoning all our affairs, our habits, our acquaintances, even our friends, to head off to some enchanted isle, to live without worries, without aggravations, obligations and, above all, without newspapers?

One could say, seriously, that journalism, that first and last of things, as Aesop would have deemed it, has created a new way of life, full of progress, advantages and anxieties. This voice of humanity, to which we awake each morning, explains to us how the rest of the world has fared the day previously. It as soon proclaims great truths, as outrageous lies, but always keeps track of our collective life at all hours of the day or night. Is it not a marvel, despite all the flaws and miseries to be found within its pages?

While newspapers are necessary for gleaning our collective thought and actions, is it not also shocking and horrifying to see it all in such detail? There is fighting everywhere, and weeks and months of threats and injury pass without a single issue being resolved, indeed without even any progress towards a solution being made. Besides, while we wait for an outcome, we are subjected to such meticulous detail of each phase of a conflict that it appears to have lasted much longer. Is it not surprising then that we artists, who do not have our hands upon the helm of history, often wish to find a quiet part of the vessel in which to sleep, and not to reawaken, until some years hence, when we can greet the new world into which we will have been carried?

Yes, truthfully, if we could only do that, if we could only abstain from collective life, and isolate ourselves from all politics for a while, we would be surprised, on returning to the world, at the progress that would have been achieved out of our sight. However, this gift has not been given us, and when we flee from the field of action, seeking to put everything out of our minds, and searching for rest among a people whose pace of life is slower, and whose spirit is less ardent than ours, we only find horrors that we did not expect, and end up regretting having left behind the present for the past, the living for the dead.

So there you have it; this will be the text of my discourse, and is the reason why I am bothering to write at all, even though it is not such an agreeable task. I promised myself, at the beginning, to keep my personal impressions to myself as much as possible; but I now feel that keeping this pledge would be indolent cowardice, and I retract my promise.

CHAPTER FIVE

e arrived in Palma in November 1838, to a heat comparable with our month of June. A fortnight before, we had left an extremely cold Paris and it was a great pleasure for us, after having felt the first assaults of winter, to leave the enemy behind. To this delight can be added that of visiting a city of such great character, possessing several first rate buildings of historical and aesthetic interest.

However, we soon began to worry about the problems of establishing ourselves there, and before long we realised that the Spaniards who had recommended Majorca to us as the most hospitable country, with the most inexhaustible resources, had been deluding themselves, as well as us. In a land so close to the great civilisations of Europe we had not expected to encounter such difficulties in finding a single hostelry. This absence of lodgings for travellers should have made us see, in itself, what Majorca was really like in comparison with the rest of the world, and should have made us decide to return immediately to Barcelona, where, at least, we had access to a dreadful hostel called, emphatically, the *Four Nations Hotel.*

In Palma, it is necessary to have been recommended and announced to at least twenty or more noteworthy people, and to have given some months notice of your arrival, before having any hope of not having to sleep out in the cold. The only thing it was possible for them to offer us was two small furnished rooms, perhaps bare rooms would be more accurate, in a shady district, where strangers were to consider themselves lucky to have found a bed with straps, a mattress that was as soft and flexible as slate, a cane chair and a place where the menu consisted largely of peppers and garlic.

In less than an hour we were convinced that if we did not show ourselves delighted with our reception, the locals would give us black looks, as if we were trouble makers or disrespectful types, or at the very least they would look on us with sympathy as if we were lunatics. Woe betide the poor person who is not completely satisfied with everything in Spain! The slightest grimace you might make on finding vermin in your bed, or scorpions in your soup, would bring the deepest scorn upon your head and stir up universal indignation against you. Consequently, we kept our complaints to ourselves, and slowly began to comprehend the source of this lack of resources and this apparent lack of hospitality.

Apart from the habitual lack of activity or energy of the Majorcans, the civil war, which had turned the country upside down for some time, had interrupted all movement in those days between the population of the island and that of the continent. Majorca had become the refuge of as many Spaniards as the island could hold, and the indigenous people, retrenched in their homes, did their best not to leave them, risking adventure and hard knocks in the motherland.

To these reasons one must add the total absence of industry, and also the customs office, which imposed exorbitant duties on items essential to the general welfare.[1]

Palma is capable of housing a certain number of inhabitants; as the population swells, space gets tighter. Hardly any new building takes place; and in their

---

[1] For a piano that we wanted to bring in from France, they demanded 700 francs entry duty, which almost coincided with the value of the instrument. We then wished to return it to France, but this was not permitted; leave it in the port until further instructions, not allowed; ensure that it did not pass through the city (we were then living in the country) so as to avoid port charges, which are different from import duties, that was against the law; leave it in town so as to avoid departure charges, which are different from arrival charges, this was impossible; at one point we only wished to throw it into the sea, although it was not clear if we even had the right to do that.
After a fortnight's negotiations we arranged for it to be taken out of one city gate rather than another and that way we only ended up paying around 400 francs. (Author's Note)

dwellings, nothing is renewed. Except, perhaps, in the houses of one or two families, most of the furniture has not been changed in two hundred years. They are not familiar with the fashion empire, the need for luxury, or for life's little comforts. There is apathy on the one hand and difficulty on the other, and so it continues. There are the bare essentials, but absolutely nothing superfluous. Thus, hospitality is limited to mere words.

There is a phrase that is used in Majorca, as in the rest of Spain, to excuse lending anything; this consists in offering everything: *The house and all its contents are at your disposition.* You cannot even look at a painting, touch a piece of fabric, or lift up a chair without someone saying, with perfect grace: *It is at your disposition.* But beware of accepting even a pin, because that would be a gross indiscretion.

I committed an impertinence of this type on my arrival in Palma, and I believe I shall never be rehabilitated in the eyes of the Marquis de ***[2]. I came highly recommended to this young Palman *lion* and I believed I could accept his offer of his coach to take a ride around the town. He had offered it to me so considerately! However, the following morning, I received a card from him leaving me in no doubt that I had broken all convention, and I returned the vehicle to him promptly, without ever having made use of it.

I did find exceptions to this rule, but these were from people who had travelled and who knew something of the

---

[2] Monsieur le Marquis de la Bastide (Editor's note).

world and were, to a certain extent, truly citizens of the globe. If others, out of the goodness of their hearts, inclined towards consideration and frankness, nobody (it is absolutely necessary to stress this in order to be able to grasp the dire straits that the customs house and the lack of industry have brought upon such a rich land), nobody would have offered us a corner of their house, without imposing so many conditions and impediments that we would have had to be really indiscreet to have accepted.

We were able to understand the impossible situation in which they find themselves when we were seeking to settle in ourselves. It was impossible to find a single habitable room in the entire city.

An apartment in Palma consists of four absolutely bare walls, without doors or windows. In the majority of bourgeois homes they do not use glass; and when one wishes to acquire this delicacy, so essential in winter, one must have the frames made up as well. Each tenant, when they move (and they usually do not move much), takes with him the windows, the locks and even the door hinges. His successor is obliged to begin by replacing them, unless that is he cares to live with draughts, a liking to be found all over Palma.

It would take at least six months to have not only the doors and windows made, but also the beds, the tables and the chairs, in short, everything, no matter how simple and primitive the furnishings. There are very few workmen, and none of them show any signs of hurrying; besides, they lack materials and tools. A Majorcan always has an excuse to avoid rushing. "Life is so long! You must be French," (that is to say extravagant and fanatical), "to wish to have something done in a hurry. If you have waited six months, why not wait another six? And if you are not content with the country, then why do you stay? Do we need your presence here? We got on fine without you. Do you think you are going to change the way things are done? Not a chance! Listen, we let people have their say, and then we do things our way."

"But is there nothing we can hire?"

"Hire? What is that? Rent furniture? Do you think there is enough to spare that we can hire it out?"

"Then is there nothing we can buy?"

"Buy? That's all we need, finished items in stock. Do you think we have time to spare to make furniture in advance? If you want something, have it sent from France. They've got everything there!"

"But having things sent from France would mean a six months wait, at least, and we would have to pay import duties. Do you mean that if one has been foolish enough to come here, the only remedy is to leave?"

"That is what I would advise you. Either that or have patience, a lot of patience; *mucha calma*!" That is Majorcan wisdom.

We were about to follow this advise when, surely with the best of intentions, they did us the dubious favour of finding us a house in the country to hire.

It was the villa of a rich bourgeois who, for a very moderate price, for us, but quite high for the locals (some one hundred francs a month), rented us the entire house. It was furnished, like all the second residences in the country, with beds having straps, rather than springs, or wooden beds painted green, some formed by two trestles upon which two boards were placed and a thin mattress. The walls were bare and whitewashed and, as an added luxury, there were windows with glass in them in nearly all of the rooms. Finally, for decoration, in the room known as the parlour, there were four horrendous drawings over the chimneypiece, like those you would find in the most humble cottage in one of our villages, and which Señor Gomez, our landlord, had had the naiveté to carefully frame as if they were precious works of art. As for the rest, the house was large, airy (too airy), well distributed, and located in a pleasant spot at the foot of some low mountains whose sides were rounded and fertile. We were at one end of a productive valley, the other end of which terminated in the yellow walls of Palma, the enormous mass of the cathedral, and the shimmering sea on the horizon.

Our first days in that retreat were spent in sweet, aimless wandering around the area enjoying the delicious climate and the charms of the local nature, which were all new for us.

Despite having spent a great deal of my life travelling, I had never been very far from my country. It was, therefore, the first time that I had seen a terrain and vegetation so essentially different from those in our more temperate latitudes. When I first saw Italy, I stepped ashore on the Tuscan coast and the grandiose idea I had formed of that landscape impeded me from enjoying the pastoral beauty and the agreeable charm of the area. On the banks of the Arno, I believed myself on those of the Indre, and I travelled as far as Venice without being astounded by anything. But there was no familiar landscape with which I could compare Majorca. The people, the houses, the plants and even the very pebbles on the lanes had a unique character. My children were so impressed that they started to collect everything and tried to fill our trunks with beautiful chunks of quartz and multi-coloured veined marble, taken from the dry stone walls which surrounded every enclosure. Some of the local peasants, seeing us pick up everything, even dead branches, took us for apothecaries, while others looked upon us as if we were complete lunatics.

CHAPTER SIX

he island owes its great variety of forms to the perpetual movement of a ground that has been fashioned and warped by cataclysms since the world began. The part where we then lived, known as the *Establiments*, enclosed, within a horizon of a few leagues, some very diverse scenery.

On the fertile slopes surrounding us, all the cultivation was carried out on large terraces scattered throughout the hills. This cultivation in terraces, adopted throughout the island, continually threatened by the rains and flash floods that hurtle down seasonal rivers, is very favourable for trees, and it gives the countryside the appearance of an admirably cared for orchard.

To our right, the hills progressively rose up beyond the smoothly sloping pasturage to the fir covered mountains. At the foot of these mountains there flowed, in winter, and after summer storms, a seasonal river, that when we arrived was a mere dry bed of disordered shingle. However, the beautiful moss that covered those stones, the little bridges stained green with damp, cracked by the violence of past currents and half hidden among the branches that hung down from the willows and the poplars, whose attractive, slender, leafy branches leaned together to form an interlaced canopy of green from one bank to the other, the fine trickle of water that flowed noiselessly among reeds and myrtles, and the ever present group of children, women and goats squatting along those mysterious banks, all combined to make the site an admirable subject for painters. Every day we strolled along this dry river bed, and we nicknamed this patch of the landscape the *Land of Pousin*, because this section of wild nature, elegant and proud in its melancholy, reminded us of the places which that grand maestro appears to have particularly cherished.

A couple of hundred paces from our hermitage, the dry river divided into a number of tributaries and its course appeared to lose itself in the plain. Olive and carob trees joined their branches together over the toiled earth and gave that cultivated area something of the air of a forest.

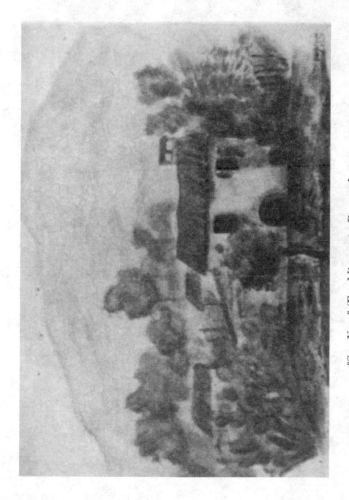

"Son Vent" (Establiments) - Peasant's cottage
(Drawing by Maurice Sand)

Bellver Castle
(Drawing by Parcerisa)

Throughout the hillocks that encircle this afforested area, are built cottages that are grand in style but truly Lilliputian in scale. It is difficult to imagine how many barns, sheds, stables, corrals and gardens a *pages* (a land owning peasant) could accumulate in an acre of land, and what unconscious, innate taste presides over this erratic disposition. The cottages usually have two storeys, and a virtually flat roof whose overhanging eaves offer some shade to a gallery with openings on all sides like a row of merlons topped by a Florentine roof. This symmetric crowning gives an appearance of splendour and strength to even the frailest and pitiable of buildings, and the enormous clusters of corn cobs and peppers drying in the open air, suspended between each opening in the gallery, form a weighty garland of alternating red and amber whose effect is incredibly rich and endearing. The cottage is usually surrounded by a great fence of cacti or prickly pear, whose bizarre fleshy leaves merge together into a wall which provides protection from the cold winds for the frail shelters made of seaweed and reeds where ewes are kept. As these peasants never steal from each other, they have nothing more than a gate of the same material to close off their property. Their allotments, where almost no vegetables, except tomatoes and peppers, are grown, are usually surrounded by groups of almond and orange trees. The colours of all of this are magnificent and often, to put the finishing touch to the wondrous tableau that the cottage and its grounds form, you will find a single palm tree in the midst of it all unfolding its graceful parasol or leaning against the side of the building like some beautiful headdress with an egret's feather.

This region is one of the most flourishing on the island, and the rationale that M. Grasset de Saint-Sauveur gives in his *Voyage to the Balearic Isles*, confirms what I have said about the scarcity of cultivation, in general, on Majorca. The remarks that this imperial bureaucrat made in 1807, with regard to the apathy and ignorance of the Majorcan *pages*, led him to investigate the causes. He found two main ones.

The first was the large number of monasteries and convents that absorbed a great many of this already restricted population. This inconvenience has now disappeared thanks to Señor Mendizabal's forthright decree, which the devout on Majorca will never forgive him for.

The second is the servile mentality that dominates the populace and leads them to enter the service of the rich and the aristocracy in droves. That abuse is still very much alive. Every Majorcan nobleman has a large retinue that his income barely allows him to maintain, despite the fact that it brings him little apparent benefit; it would be impossible to be worse served than by that gaggle of honorary servants. If one has ever wondered on what could a rich Majorcan spend his income, in a country without luxuries or temptations of any kind, one need only look for answer at any country estate to find it full of filthy idlers of both sexes who occupy the parts of the building reserved for their use and who, once they have spent a year in the service of their lord, have the right to lodging, clothing and victuals for life. Those who wish to leave service may do so by renouncing some of their privileges. However, tradition still allows them to return, every morning, to take a cup of chocolate with their former colleagues and to take part, like Sancho in Camacho's house, in all of the bean feasts organised on the estate.

At first glance, these traditions would appear to be patriarchal and one is tempted to admire the republican sentiment that presides over this relationship of master to servant, but then one realises that it is republicanism in the style of ancient Rome, and that these servants are chained, through laziness or poverty, to the vanity of their masters. It is a luxury on Majorca to have fifteen domestics for a type of house that needs no more than two at most. When one sees vast uncultivated tracts, lost industries and all hope of progress held back by ineptitude and nonchalance, I do not know who to despise more, the master who encourages and perpetuates this self-abasement of his fellow men, or the slave who prefers a degrading life of leisure rather than labour, through which he would recuperate his independence and human dignity.

However, it has happened that in response to increases in their expenditures and a decrease in their incomes, some rich Majorcan proprietors have decided to seek a remedy for the negligence of their estates and the penury of their workers. They have sold part of their lands on lifelong leases to the peasants. M. Grassett de Saint-Sauver notes that on all the great estates where this experiment has been carried out, the land, which had previously appeared to be barren, has begun to produce with such abundance in the hands of men with a vested interest in its improvement, that in a few years the two parties to the contract will surely be more than satisfied with the arrangement.

M. Grasset's predictions have been fulfilled completely and today the *Establiments* region, among others, has become one huge vegetable garden; the population has increased, numerous homes have been built on the hillocks and the peasants have acquired a certain ease which, although it has not yet enlightened them, has given them a greater propensity to work. It will take years before the Majorcan becomes an active and conscientious worker; and he may well have to pass through that painful phase, like us, in which individual greed drives everything, before he reaches the point where he can understand that that is not the goal of humanity either. Meanwhile, we can leave him his guitar and his rosary with which to kill time. Surely a better fate than ours awaits these immature civilisations, which one day we will start off on the road to true civilisation, without throwing in their faces all that we will have done for them. They are not yet sufficiently developed to be exposed to the revolutionary storms that have raged over our heads since we comprehended our perfectibility. France, alone, ignored, ridiculed and fought by the rest of the world, has made giant strides, yet the noise of our titanic struggles has still not woken from their slumber those smaller populations who sleep so profoundly in the cradle of the Mediterranean, within reach of our cannons. A day will come in which we will confer on them the baptism of true liberty and they will sit at the banquet like workers taken on at the last minute[1]. We will find the key to our social destiny, we will fulfil our most exalted dreams; and while the nations that surround us slowly drift into our revolutionary church, these impecunious islanders, whose weakness leaves them prey to the nations that dispute their ownership, will present themselves at our communion.

While awaiting that day in which we, the first in Europe, will proclaim the law of equality for all men, and independence for all peoples, the world remains governed by the law of the strongest in war, or that of the most cunning in diplomacy; human rights are mere words and the fate of all isolated and restricted populations,

like the Transylvanian, the Turk or the Hungarian,[2]

is to be devoured by the victor. If this were always to be thus, I would not wish for Spain, or England, or even France, to be Majorca's tutor, and I would care as little for its fate as I do for the strange civilisation that we are exporting to Africa.

---

[1] Refers to the tradition that seasonal workers employed in the last few days of a harvest were still invited to the celebratory harvest feast. (Tr. Note)

[2] La Fontaine, the fable of *The Thieves and the Ass*

CHAPTER SEVEN

e had been in *Establiments* for three weeks when the rains began. Up to that time we had had wonderful weather; the lemon trees and the myrtles had still been in flower and, in the first days of December, I had remained out in the open air on a terrace until five o'clock in the morning, enjoying the benefit of a delectable temperature. In this I am a good barometer, since I do not know of anyone who feels the cold as terribly as I, and enthusiasm for nature is not capable of rendering me insensible to the least chill. However, apart from the charm of a moonlit landscape and the scent of the flowers that I could detect,

my sleepless night was not very exciting. I was not there as a poet, seeking inspiration, but rather as an idler, merely listening and contemplating. I remember being most entertained by noting the noises of the night and attempting to identify them.

It is commonly accepted that each country has its harmonies, its laments, its cries and its mysterious whispers, and this material language of objects is not the least of the characteristic signs that impress the traveller. The mysterious lapping of water against cold marble walls, the slow and measured pace of the watchmen along the quay, the sharp, almost childlike cry of the field rats chasing and fighting one another over the muddy paving stones, in short all of the furtive and singular noises that barely perturb the melancholy silence of a night in Venice, cannot compare with the monotonous sound of the sea, the *¿quien vive?*[1] of the guard and the melancholy wail of the *serenos*[2] of Barcelona. Lake Maggiore has different harmonies than the lake of Geneva. The incessant snap and crackle of pine cones in the forests of Switzerland does not resemble in the least the snap and crackle one may hear among glaciers.

The silence in Majorca is more profound than anywhere else in the world. Occasionally, the donkeys and the mules, which spend the night grazing, interrupt the serenity by shaking their bells, but the sound is higher-pitched and more melodic than the cowbells of

---

[1] Who goes there? (Tr.)

[2] Night-watchmen (Tr.)

Switzerland. Boleros can be heard in even the most remote places and on the darkest nights. There is not a peasant there who does not have a guitar that they always play late into the evening. From my terrace, one could also hear the sea, but at such a distance and so faintly that I was reminded of that strangely fantastic and memorable poem the Djinns:

> I listen
> Everything flees.
> Doubt
> Night
> Everything passes.
> Space
> Effaces
> Noise.

In a neighbouring farm I heard a baby cry, and also heard its mother, who to lull it back to sleep sang a beautiful local folk song that sounded very sad and very Arabic. But I also heard other, less poetic, voices to remind me of the more vulgar side of Majorca.

The pigs awake, protesting in a manner I find hard to describe. Then the *pages*, the father of the family, hearing his cherished pigs, awakes, like the mother who had been awoken earlier by the cry of her baby. I hear him pop his head out of the window and berate the inhabitants of the neighbouring stall in an authoritarian voice. The pigs appear to understand him well, because they soon become silent. Then the peasant, apparently to help him return to his slumber, can be heard reciting the rosary in a lugubrious voice, which, as he resists the sleep that steals upon him, rises and falls like the murmur of distant waves. From time to time the pigs let out some savage cry and the peasant raises his voice without interrupting his prayer and the docile animals, calmed by an *Ora pro nobis* or an *Ave Maria* declaimed thus, become silent at once. As for the child, he has doubtless listened to it all with open eyes, lost in that stupor into which unidentifiable noises plunge the thoughts of the recently born in their cradles, thoughts which mysteriously organise themselves prior to revealing intelligence.

Then, after so many serene nights, the deluge began. One morning, after the wind had spent the entire night in long howls that shook the house, the rain began to lash against our windows, and we heard, on arising, the noise of rushing water, as a torrent dashed among the stones of the river bed seeking the sea. The next day it was even louder and on the following it rolled the rocks impeding its passage out of its way. All of the blossom in the trees had fallen, and the rain streamed into our poorly sealed rooms.

It is difficult to understand why the Majorcans take so few precautions against the lashing of the wind and the rain. Their delusion or bravado is so exalted that they totally disavow the adventitious, but serious, inclemencies of their climate. Until the very end of the two months of deluge we had to face, the locals still maintained that it never rained in Majorca. Had we observed beforehand the position of the mountain peaks and the general direction of the wind, we would have been prepared in advance for the inevitable suffering that awaited us.

Yet another adversity was reserved for us, which I have mentioned briefly above when I started to recount my journey from its end. One of our party became ill. Of a very delicate constitution and subject to a serious irritation of the larynx, he soon began to feel the effects of the damp. The villa we were renting from Señor Gomez, called *Son Vent* (Windy House), in the local dialect, soon became uninhabitable. The walls were so thin that in our bedrooms the whitewash began to swell up like a sponge. I myself had never experienced such cold, although, in fact, the temperatures were not all that low, it was just that we were accustomed to warming ourselves in winter and that house without a chimney was like a blanket of ice wrapped around our shoulders that left me feeling paralysed.

We could not become accustomed to the asphyxiating stench of the *brasers*[3] and our poor invalid began to suffer and cough.

From this moment on, we became an object of horror

---

[3] Round pan-like braziers that were filled with smouldering charcoal or turf and placed underneath a round table. A thick, overhanging tablecloth would keep in the heat from this device, which would then heat the legs of those sat at the table. *Brasers* are still available in Spain, although today they are usually powered by electricity. (Tr. Note)

and fear for the entire local population. They considered us affected with, and carriers of, pulmonary tuberculosis, only comparable to the plague within the *contagionist*[4] prejudices of Spanish medicine. A rich physician, who deigned to visit us, for the modicum sum of 45 Francs, declared that it was nothing and did not prescribe anything for it. His assistant, who we had nicknamed *Malvavisco* on account of his favourite prescription,[5] was so filthy, that our invalid was reluctant to even let him take his pulse.

Another doctor obligingly came to our aid, but the pharmacy in Palma was so poorly stocked that we could only obtain some detestable drugs from that quarter. Besides, the illness appeared to worsen, due to causes that no amount of science or care could have combated with efficiency.

One morning, when we had become seriously concerned about the duration of the rains and our companion's sufferings, which were clearly linked, we received a letter from the bombastic Señor Gomez telling us, in full Spanish style, that we had with us a person whose illness he, Don Gomez (the dirtiest, ugliest man on the entire planet), found repugnant. He added that as we were contaminating his home, and that as this was

---

4 (*Italics mine*). French revolutionary science, while advanced in many ways, dismissed the idea of "the germ theory"; an attitude analogous to Stalinist Russia's rejection of tectonic plates or Hitler's rejection of nuclear physics. These ideas being rejected because they were seen as somehow counter to the prevailing political orthodoxy. (Tr. Note)

5 An infusion of marshmallow (Author's Note)

something that could affect his family's expected life-span, he was asking us to leave his villa with as little delay as possible.

We did not regret having to move, we had already decided that we could not stay there for much longer without fear of drowning in our beds. However, our invalid was in no fit state to be moved without danger, above all with the means of transport available on Majorca, and with the prevailing weather. Then there was the difficulty of knowing where to go, since rumour of our "consumption" had spread instantly and we knew we would not easily find asylum anywhere, even for gold, and even for a single night. We also knew well that people who had offered to take us in earlier would not be free from this prejudice, and that had we approached them we would have infected them with the reprobation that hung over us. Without the hospitality of the French consul, who worked miracles to welcome us all under his roof, we would have been threatened with camping in some cave, like true Bohemians.

Another miracle then happened, and we found asylum for the winter. In the Carthusian monastery at Valldemosa, there was a Spanish refugee who had hidden himself there for who knows what political reason. When we had visited the monastery (the poetry of which had gone to my head), we had been impressed by his distinction and his manners, the melancholy beauty of his wife, and with the rustic, but comfortable, furniture in his cell. As it happens, this mysterious couple wished to leave the country in a hurry, and were as glad to leave us their furniture and their cell as we were to secure them. For the modest sum of a thousand francs, then, we took possession of an entire household, that in France would have cost us a mere hundred ecus, the basic necessities in Majorca being so limited, costly and difficult to find.

As we then spent four days in Palma, although this time without moving very much from the fireplace that, luckily, the consul possessed (the deluge continued), I will interrupt my narrative a little to give a description of the Majorcan capital. M. Laurens, who explored it and drew its more beautiful aspects in the following year, shall be the guide I will now introduce to the reader, since he is a far more competent archaeologist than I.

PART TWO

CHAPTER ONE

lthough Majorca was occupied by the Moors for four hundred years, very few traces of that period remain. In Palma, this is confined to a small bathhouse.

Nothing remains of the Romans; and of the Carthaginians only some ruins near the ancient capital of Alcudia. M. Grasset de Saint-Sauveur attributes the tradition that Hannibal was born here to the boastfulness of the Majorcans, although this story may contain a grain of verisimilitude.[1]

The Moorish influence has been perpetuated in even

---

[1] The Majorcans maintain that Hamilcar, voyaging from Africa to Catalonia with his pregnant wife, stopped at a point on the island where a temple had been built dedicated to Lucina, and that Hannibal had been born there. This same tale appears in *The History of Majorca* by Dameto. (Grasset de Saint-Sauveur). [Author's note].

the most insignificant building. However, it required Monsieur Laurens to rectify the archaeological errors of his predecessors, before ignorant travellers, like myself, could realise that they were not stumbling upon genuine vestiges of Arab architecture at every step.

"In Palma," says M. Laurens, I have not seen buildings of a very ancient construction. The most interesting structures, both in terms of their architecture and their age, all belong to the early 16th century; but the graceful, and brilliant, art of that epoch does not manifest itself in the same way there as in France.

"Above the ground floor, these houses have only a first floor, and a very low granary.[2] Access to the street consists of a plain arch; but its sheer size and the number of dressed stones radiating out from it in long spokes give the whole structure great presence. Light enters the large rooms on the first floor through high windows, divided by extremely thin columns that give them a completely Arabic appearance.

"This characteristic is so pronounced, that I had to examine more than twenty identically constructed houses and study every aspect of their construction before being convinced that those windows had not been taken from the walls of some truly fabulous Moorish palace, of which the Alhambra in Grenada is the best surviving example.

"I have never encountered anywhere else but in Majorca six foot high columns that are a mere three

---

[2] They are not in fact granaries, but drying areas, known locally as *porchos*. (Author's note).

inches in diameter. The refinement of the marble from which they are made, the taste shown in the capital at the top, all of this would have led me to surmise an Arabic origin. Small matter, these copies are certainly as attractive as the originals.

"The granary that makes up the top floor is a gallery, or rather a series of connected windows copied exactly from those that crown the *Lonja*. Finally, there is the overhanging roof, sustained by artistically carved beams, which protect this floor from the rain and the sun, and produce the most charming effects of light, thanks to the long shadows it projects onto the house, and the contrast of the dark brown shapes of the frame and the brilliant tones of the sky.

"The stairway, very tastefully worked, is to be found in the interior of a courtyard at the centre of the house and separated from the street entrance by a vestibule, in which can be seen some pilasters with capitals adorned with sculpted leaves, or with a shield held up by angels.

"For more than a century after the Renaissance, the Majorcans built their private houses with great luxury. Although following the same distribution, they added the changes of taste, which should have been represented by changes in the architecture, to the vestibules and stairways. Thus, throughout the island, Tuscan and Doric columns, and banisters and balustrades, that always bestow something of a sumptuous appearance on the abodes of the aristocracy, can be seen.

"This predilection for ornamenting the stairways, as

well as echoes of Arabic taste, can also be found in the humblest of dwellings, even when a single stairway leads directly from the street to the first floor. In that case, each step is covered with ceramic tiles painted with brilliant blue, yellow or red flowers."

This description is very accurate and M. Laurens' drawings admirably reproduce the elegance of those interiors, whose peristyle would furnish our theatres with a beautiful, and extremely simple, element of decoration.

These small paved courtyards, often surrounded by columns like the *cortile* of Venetian palaces, usually have a well, in a very pure style, that befits its surroundings. They do not share the aspect of our dirty, and bare, courtyards, nor are they used for the same purpose. You will never find there the entrance to a stable, or coach house. They are true inner courts, which perhaps echo the atrium of the Romans. One finds there, in some shape or form, the *prothyrum* and the *cavoedium*; the well in the middle obviously taking on the role of the *impluvium*.

When these peristyles are decorated with flower pots and reed matting, they look both elegant, and yet severe. Their poetry is not appreciated in the least by the Majorcan aristocracy, who are always apologising for the age of their houses, and if you profess to admire the style, they smile, assuming that you are laughing at them, or else they secretly dismiss the excessive courtesy of the French.

However, not everything in an aristocratic Majorcan

residence is equally poetic. There are certain unhygienic details that I would find very embarrassing to convey to my reader, unless, as Jacquemont notes, when referring to Indian habits, I were to finish my letter in Latin.

Not knowing enough Latin, I will recommend, to the curious, a passage that M. Grasset de Saint-Saveur, a less formal writer than M. Laurens, but very truthful on this issue, devoted to the pantries of Majorca, and many of the older houses in Spain and Italy. Especially notable in this passage is an extremely strange Spanish medical prescription that is still ubiquitous throughout Majorca.[3]

The interior of these palaces does not resemble the exteriors in the least. There is nothing more revealing, both of nations and individuals, than the disposition of furniture in their homes.

In Paris, where the whims of fashion and the abundance of industrial products lead to a barely credible variety within apartments, it is unquestionable that one only has to enter the house of a well-to-do person to get an idea of his character. In the blink of an eye, one can note whether he has taste, or is orderly, avaricious or neglectful, whether he has a methodical or novelistic spirit, and whether he is hospitable or ostentatious.

Like everybody else, I have my systems for making such judgements, which does not prevent me from regularly erring in my deductions, as happens to so many others.

I am particularly horrified by a room that is barely

_____
[3] See Grasset de Saint-Saveur, p-119 (Author's note).

furnished, but very tidy. Unless we are dealing with a person of great intelligence, and a large heart, completely beyond considerations of minor material things, who lives there as if it were a tent, I would take the owner to have an empty head and a cold heart.

I do not understand how, when one lives within four walls, one does not feel the need to fill the space, if only with logs and baskets, and to have something living there, even if it is only a humble potted plant, or a poor sparrow.

Emptiness and immobility make me freeze with fear, symmetry and rigorous order fill me with sadness; and if my imagination could truly picture eternal damnation, my idea of hell would surely be to live eternally in certain provincial houses where perfect order reigns, where nothing is ever out of place, where nothing lies on the floor, where nothing is used or broken, and where no animal ever enters, under the pretext that animate things spoil inanimate objects. Let every carpet in the world be ruined, if the only condition for enjoying them is that a child, a dog, or a cat, may never be seen to set foot or paw upon them.

This rigid cleanliness does not come from a genuine love of wholesomeness, but rather from an excessive laziness, or a distasteful thrift. With a little more care and activity, the *housewife*, whose tastes agree with mine, can maintain the inside of her house clean, as indeed I myself insist on accomplishing.

However, what can one say and think of the habits

and ideas of a family whose home is kept empty and immobile, without having the excuse, or the pretext, of cleanliness?

If, as I said earlier, one can easily err in one's private perceptions, it is difficult to be wrong in more general perceptions. The character of a people manifests itself as much in their clothing, and in their furniture, as in their features and their language.

Having chased all over Palma in pursuit of somewhere to live, I entered quite a number of houses. They were all so nearly identical that I feel I can deduce that their occupants shared a general character. I did not enter into any of those interiors without feeling my heart heavy with disgust or revulsion, just at seeing those bare walls, the tarnished and dusty tiles, and the sparse and dirty furniture. Everything spoke of indifference and inaction; there was never a book in sight, nor evidence of feminine labour. The men do not read, and the women do not even sew. The only real indication that anyone lives there is the smell of garlic that reveals activity from the kitchen; and the only evidence of leisure is the cigar butts scattered all over the floors.

This absence of intellectual life gives the home a dead, and empty, atmosphere that has no equivalence among us, and that makes the Majorcan resemble more an African than a European.

In all of these houses, generation succeeds generation, without transforming anything of their surroundings, and without leaving any individual impression on the things that make up our daily existence. This makes these buildings more like caravanserai than true homes; more like places where nomads camp to indifferently pass away the night, rather than the nests we try to build for our families. People who know Spain well have told me it is generally the same throughout the Peninsula.

As I have mentioned earlier, the peristyle or *atrium* of the palaces of the *cavallers* (as the patricians of Majorca are still known) have a grand, hospitable character, and even hint at comfort. But once you have climbed the elegant staircase and penetrated into the interior of the houses, you get the impression of entering a place only designed for having a siesta. Large rooms, generally in the shape of elongated squares, very high, very dark, very cold, all whitewashed and without ornamentation, huge ancient portraits of ancestors hanging in a single row; so dark, and so high up that it is impossible to distinguish any features; four or five greasy, worm-eaten, leather chairs with large golden nail heads around the edges that have not been polished in two hundred years; some Valencian mats; or some long haired sheep skins scattered hither and thither across the floors; large windows high up in the wall, covered with thick drapes; wide wooden doors of black oak, like the joists, and at times an ancient curtain with the family coat of arms richly embroidered, but faded and moth-eaten; this is how these Majorcan palaces are on the inside. The only tables on view are those on which the family eats; glass window panes are very rare and occupy such little space on those immense panels, which let in very little light indeed.

The master of the house can be found, standing and smoking, in profound silence; the mistress sat in a great chair, fanning herself and thinking of nothing. The children are never to be seen: they live with the servants, in the kitchen or the attic, I know not; the parents do not concern themselves with them. A chaplain comes and goes, without achieving anything. The twenty or thirty servants take a siesta, while an ancient maid risks opening the door, when the visitor has knocked fifteen times.

This life is not void of a certain *character*, as we would say within the unlimited sense we allow that word today; but if one condemned the calmest of our bourgeoisie to live thus, they would surely become lunatic from desperation, or a demagogue through a reaction of their spirit.

CHAPTER TWO

he three principal buildings in Palma are the cathedral, the Lonja (exchange), and the Royal Palace.

The cathedral, attributed by the Majorcans to James the Conqueror, their first Christian king and their local version of Charlemagne, was in fact initiated during his reign, but it was not finished until 1601. It is of an immense bareness; constructed entirely in a fine grained limestone, of a beautiful amber colour.

This imposing mass, which rises directly off the shoreline, is most impressive when approached from the sea, though in terms of taste, the only aspect of real worth is the southern portal, which M. Laurens observes to be the most beautiful specimen of gothic art that he has had occasion to draw. The interior is very stern, and gloomy.

The winds off the sea once penetrated the interior with some fury through the great openings in the main entrance, and were known to have blown pictures off the walls, or even blown the chalice over in the middle of a mass. Consequently, the doors and the rose windows on that side of the building were sealed off. The nave is, at least, five hundred and forty palms[1] long, by three hundred and seventy wide.

In the middle of the choir stalls, there is a simple marble sarcophagus which is opened up for foreigners to display the mummified remains of James the Second, the son of the Conqueror, a devout prince as weak, and as peaceful, as his father was forceful, and warlike.

The Majorcans maintain that their cathedral is superior to that of Barcelona, and that their *Lonja* is infinitely more beautiful than that of Valencia. I cannot verify the latter point, but as for the former, it is unsustainable.

In both cathedrals, there is a singular trophy that also adorns the majority of towns in Spain: it is the hideous head of a Moor in painted wood, wearing a turban, which finishes off the pendentive of the organ. This representation of a severed head is often shown with a long white beard, and is painted red underneath, to symbolise the impure blood of the vanquished.

The keystones of the arches in the nave display numerous coats of arms. To have your family crest in the

---

[1] The Spanish *palmo* is the *pan* used as a measurement in our southern provinces. (Author's note). It is equivalent to the English "hands" traditionally used to measure horses. (Tr. Note).

house of God was a singular privilege, for which the knights of Majorca paid dear; thanks to this levy on vanity, it proved possible to complete the cathedral in a century in which devotion to the church had cooled, somewhat. It would be unjust to attribute this weakness only to the Majorcans; it was a vanity shared by many devout nobles of the period, throughout the world.

The Lonja is the building that impressed me the most, both for its elegant proportions, and the originality that characterises it, which however, did not preclude an absolute regularity, or a tasteful simplicity.

This exchange was commenced, and finished, in the first half of the fifteenth century. The illustrious Jovellanos describes it in minute detail, and the *Magasin Pittoresque* popularised it with a very interesting drawing of it, published many years ago. The interior is a vast hall, sustained by six elegantly subtle, spiral-fluted columns.

The building was once used for meetings of merchants, and numerous navigators who flocked to Palma. The Lonja is witness to the splendid commercial past of Majorca; today, however, it is only used during public festivities. It must be interesting to see the Majorcans, dressed in the rich gowns of their parents, cavorting gravely in the ancient dance hall; but the rain then held us captive in the mountains, and we were unable to witness that carnival, less famous and, perhaps, less cheerless than that of Venice. As for the Lonja, although I found it beautiful, it has not come near to supplanting in my memory that precious jewel known as the *Cadoro*, the ancient mint on the Grand-Canal.

The Royal Palace of Palma, which Grasset de Saint-Sauveur, without hesitation, considers Roman and Moorish (which inspired in him emotions appropriate to the imperial style) is said to have been constructed in 1309. Laurens confesses himself perplexed by the small pairs of windows, and the enigmatic diminutive columns he studied in the building.

Would it be too audacious, perhaps, to attribute the anomalies of taste one observes in so many Majorcan buildings to the intercalation of ancient fragments into later buildings? In the same way as Renaissance tastes, in France and Italy, introduced authentic Greek and Roman medallions and bas-reliefs into their sculptural ornamentation, is it not possible that the Christians of Majorca, after having torn down all of the Moorish buildings[2], ended up using some of

---

[2] The taking and sacking of Palma by the Christians in December 1229, is described in picturesque detail in the Chronicle of Marsili (unpublished). This is a fragment:

"The thieves and bandits, when searching the Moorish houses found beautiful women, and pretty young girls, who held in their lap gold and silver coins, pearls and precious stones, golden and silver bracelets, sapphires and all kinds of precious jewels. They showed these to the armed men before them and, between bitter tears, pleaded with them in Saracen: "Take all of this, leave us only enough on which to live!"

"The greed, and excesses, of the men of the house of Aragon were such that they did not appear again before their lord for eight days, occupied as they were in finding any remaining hidden riches, in order to appropriate them for themselves.

"This reached such a point that, the following day, as there was not a cook, nor an official of the king's household to be found, an Aragonese nobleman, Ladro, said to his master:

"My Lord, let me invite you to dine with me, since we have sufficient food, and I have been told that in my rooms there is a good cow; there will we have a fine meal and there may we sleep this night."

"The king then followed this nobleman, with joy in his heart". (Author's note).

the rich debris, increasingly encrusting it into their subsequent constructions?

Whatever the truth of the matter was, the Royal Palace of Palma is a very picturesque building. I know of no other edifice as irregular, as uncomfortable, as savagely medieval, as proud, as characteristic or as *hidalgo* as this lordly mansion comprising galleries, towers, terraces and arcades clambering on top of one another up to a considerable height, and culminating in a gothic angel that, from its lofty position, looks out across the sea, towards Spain.

This palace, which houses the archives, is the residence of the *Capitan General*[3], the most eminent person on the island. This is how M. Grasset de Saint-Sauveur describes the interior:

"The first space is a kind of vestibule that serves as a guardroom. One then passes directly into two huge rooms, where there is hardly a seat to be found.

"The third space is the room where audiences are held; it contains a throne on a dais with three steps leading up to it, covered in a tapestry. The throne itself is covered in crimson velvet and bordered around the edges in gold. On each side of it are two lions in gilded wood. The canopy that covers the throne is also in crimson velvet, crowned with ostrich plumes. Above the throne are hung portraits of the King and Queen.

"This is the room in which, on days of official

---

[3] An officer with the rank of Field Marshall. He was only supreme commander during wars; otherwise the civilian governor was in charge. (Tr. Note).

business, the general receives the different civil administration bodies, the officers of the garrison or noteworthy foreigners."

The Capitan General, who also serves as the governor, for whom we had some letters, did us the honour of receiving one of us, who took charge of delivering them to him in that same room. Our companion found the high official near his throne, doubtless the same one as described by Grasset de Saint-Sauveur in 1807, since it was worn, faded, shabby and spattered with olive oil and candle wax stains. The two lions have lost nearly all of their gilt, but continue making fierce grimaces at those present. The only thing that had changed was the royal effigy: this time it was the innocent Isabel, portrayed as if on some monstrous cabaret poster, who occupied the ancient golden frame in which her august ancestors had preceded her, like the models on the easel of some apprentice painter. The governor, despite being accommodated like Hoffman's Duke of Ireneus, is a much loved man, and a very affable prince.

A fourth building worthy of mention is the palace of the *Ajuntament*[4], a work of the sixteenth century, whose style has been rightly compared with that of the palaces of Florence. The roof is notable, above all for the overhangs at the edges, like those of the Florentine palaces, or those of a Swiss chalet; but it has the peculiarity of being supported by wooden caissons with richly sculpted rosettes, alternating with tall caryatids

---

[4] Town or City Council (Tr. Note)

lying under the eaves, who do not seem happy at their task, because the majority have their faces buried in their hands, as if in tears.

I have not seen the interior of the building in which portraits of the great men of Majorca are gathered. Amongst these illustrious persons, one can see the celebrated James the Conqueror, characterised as the *King of Diamonds.* One can also see an ancient painting representing the funeral of Ramon Llull which offers a very interesting and varied series of ancient costumes worn by the innumerable members of the cortege of the enlightened Majorcan doctor. Finally, also on display in this consistorial palace is a magnificent *Saint Sebastian* by Van Dyck, the existence of which nobody in Majorca had deigned to inform me.

"Palma has a school of art," adds M. Laurens, "which has trained, in our nineteenth century alone, thirty six painters, eight sculptors, eleven architects and six engravers, all now celebrated practitioners, if one is to believe the *Dictionary of Celebrated Majorcan Artists* that has just been published by the judicious Antoni Furio." I have to confess, ingenuously, that during my stay in Palma, I did not feel myself surrounded by so many great men, and that I saw nothing that would have led me to discover their existence...

"Some rich families preserve several painting of the Spanish school... But if you browse through the shops, or enter in the house of a humble citizen, you will only find the same coloured images as are displayed for sale in our public squares, and which in France only find a home under the humble roof of some poor peasant."

The palace which Palma glorifies most is that of the Count of Montenegro, an octogenarian who was once Capitan General, one of the most illustrious, and richest, native Majorcans.

This gentleman has a library that he allowed us to visit, but where I did not open a single volume, and of which I would not have been able to say a word (the respect I have for books is somewhat akin to terror), had a learned compatriot of mine not informed me of the treasures before which I had passed indifferently, like the cock from the fable, in midst of pearls.

This compatriot[5], who lived in Catalonia and Majorca for two years in order to carry out some studies on romance languages, was kind enough to allow me to look over his notes, and also gave me permission, with unusual generosity in one so erudite, to use them at my discretion. I would not do so without first cautioning my reader that my traveller friend was as enthusiastic about all things Majorcan, as I was disappointed in them.

To explain this divergence of impressions, I should say that during my stay, the Majorcan populace were inconveniencing themselves considerably to house twenty thousand refugees from the war in Spain, and it is doubtless probable that I found Palma less habitable, and the Majorcans less disposed to welcome another

---

[5] M. Tastu, one of our most erudite linguists, is married to one of our most talented, and pure, muses with a most noble character. (Author's Note).

increase in foreigners than they had certainly been two years previously. Nevertheless, I prefer to expose myself to the disapprobation of a benevolent corrector, than to write down an impression that was not my own.

Moreover, being contradicted and reproached, in public, would make me happier than being criticised, as I have been, in private, because then the public would gain a book on Majorca that is more accurate, and much more interesting than this disjointed, and perhaps unintentionally unfair account, that I feel obliged to give.

Hence, I hope M. Tastu publishes an account of his voyage; I swear that I will read, with a happy heart, everything that might make me change my mind about the Majorcans. I met some who I wished to consider representatives of a general type, and I hope that they will have no doubt of my sentiments towards them, should a copy of this account ever fall into their hands.

So it was in M. Tastu's notes that I found, among other intellectual riches listed for Majorca, mention of the library of the Count of Montenegro, which I had browsed, a little irreverently, behind the chaplain of the house, busy as I was with examining the interior of the house of an elderly Majorcan knight bachelor; an interior that was as cheerless and solemn as none other, silently overseen by a priest.

"This library, says Tastu, was created by an uncle of the Count of Montenegro, Cardinal Antoni Despuig, an intimate friend of Pius VI.

"The learned cardinal has gathered every notable

volume from the libraries of Spain, Italy and France. Of particular note is the numismatic section and that dealing with the arts of antiquity, which are very complete, indeed.

"Among the manuscripts to be found there, is one which is very curious for lovers of calligraphy: it is a book of hours. It contains some exquisite miniatures that belong to the best epochs of art.

"The lover of heraldry will find there an armorial in which the coats of arms of the Spanish nobility are drawn in full colour. These include the families of Aragon, Majorca, the Roussillon and the Languedoc. The manuscript, which appears to be from the sixteenth century used to belong to the Dameto family, united with the Despuig family and the Montenegro. Turning its pages, one finds the coat of arms of the *Bonapart* family, from which descended our great Napoleon, and of which we obtained a facsimile that I will reproduce later...

"In this library there is also the marvellous naval chart by the Majorcan Valsequa, a manuscript from 1439, a masterpiece of calligraphy and topographical drawing, in which the miniaturist practiced his most exquisite work. This chart had belonged to Amerigo Vespucci, who had bought it at an exorbitant price, as an inscription of the period, written on the back of the chart, testifies: "*Questa ampla pelle di geographia fù pagata da Amerigo Vespucci CXXX ducati di oro di marco*".

"This precious monument to medieval geography will

be published soon to continue the Catalan-Majorcan Atlas of 1375, included in Volume XIV, Part 2 of the Notes on Academic Manuscripts from Inscriptions and Literature."

On transcribing this note, I feel my hairs stand on end, because it recalls to me a horrifying scene.

We were in that same library of Count Montenegro, and the chaplain unrolled before us the nautical chart described above, this valuable and rare monument, for which Amerigo Vespucci had paid a hundred and thirty gold ducats; and heaven knows how much Cardinal Despuig, as an antique collector, had paid for it!... when it occurred to one of the thirty, or forty servants of the house to place a cork inkwell on one of the corners of the parchment, to keep it open on the table. The inkwell was full, full to the brim!

The parchment, accustomed to being rolled up, and perhaps goaded in that moment by some malignant spirit, suddenly made an effort to roll itself back up; there was a crackle, a jolt, and it succeeded, enveloping the inkwell, which disappeared within its folds, as the manuscript regained its accustomed form, free now of any hindrance. There was a collective shout, and the chaplain became more pallid than the parchment.

The chart was then slowly unrolled, hoping against hope! Alas! The inkwell was empty! The chart was soaked, and the charming little sovereigns painted in miniature were literally sailing on a sea that was blacker than the Pont-Euxin.

Then everyone lost their head. I believe that the chaplain swooned. The servants flocked in with buckets of water, as if there were a fire; then with great wipes of sponge and scrubbing brush, they set about trying to clean the chart, removing kings, seas, isles and continents, pell-mell.

Before we could oppose this fatal zeal, the chart was already beyond hope, but not beyond remedy. Luckily, M. Tastu had already made a faithful copy of it, and thanks to that, the chart may one day be, more or less, restored, and the havoc dealt with.

However, what consternation the chaplain must have experienced, when his master was informed of the event! All of us were at least six paces from the table when the catastrophe occurred; but I am convinced that this did not stop the full weight of responsibility for the incident being laid at our door, and that this incident, imputed to some French people, did not contribute greatly to restoring French prestige on Majorca.

This tragic event prevented us from contemplating, or even seeing, any of the marvels which we had been told were contained within the Montenegro palace, whether the medal cabinet, or the antique bronzes and paintings. We were anxious to flee before the master of the house returned and, sure that we would have been accused before him, we dared not return. Thus, I have to rely on M. Tastu's notes again to divest me of my ignorance.

"Next to the Cardinal's library, there is a medal cabinet containing Celt-Iberian, Moorish, Greek,

Roman, and Medieval items; an invaluable collection, that today lies in distressing disorder, awaiting some erudite to come along to organise and classify it.

"The apartments of the Count of Montenegro are decorated with works of art in marble, or in antique bronzes, fruits of an excavation at Aricia, or bought in Rome by the Cardinal. There are also many paintings of the Spanish and Italian schools, of which more than one would not be out of place in the best galleries of Europe."

Mention must be made now of the castle of Bellver[6], the ancient residence of the Kings of Majorca, which I did not see, except from a distance, on top of the hill from which it dominates the sea with great majesty. It is an ancient fortress, and one of the harshest prisons in all of Spain.

"The existing walls," according to Laurens, "were erected at the end of the thirteenth century and represent one of the most curious examples of medieval military architecture still extant, and in good repair".

When our traveller visited it, he found nearly fifty Carlist prisoners, covered in rags and tatters, and half naked, some of whom were mere children. With noisy joy, they ate the plain boiled macaroni that was doled out of a cauldron into their mess tins. They were guarded by some soldiers who knitted stockings, a cigar in their mouths.

In those times, it was to the castle of Bellver, in fact,

---

[6] In the original French, the author hesitates between *Bellver* and *Belver* and chooses to use the latter. I have preferred to use the term by which this castle is currently known. (Tr. Note)

that prisoners who could not be accommodated in Barcelona's gaols were transferred. But those formidable doors had also been known to close upon even more illustrious captives.

It was there that Don Gaspar de Jovellanos, one of Spain's most eloquent orators and most active writers, paid the penalty for writing his celebrated pamphlet *Pan y Toros*[7]. He was detained in the *torre del homenage, cuya cuva* - states Vargas - *es la mas cruda prision"*[8]. Jovellanos dedicated his ill-won leisure there to scientifically describing the prison, and narrating the story of the tragic happenings for which it had provided a backdrop in the period of the wars of the middle ages.

The Majorcans also owe an excellent description of the cathedral and the Lonja to his stay on the island. In brief, his *Letters on Majorca* are among the best documents one might consult.

During the parasitical reign of the Prince of Peace, the same dungeon that Jovellanos occupied would shortly afterwards hold another notable scientist and politician.

The following little known anecdote, from the life of a man as celebrated in France as Jovellanos is in Spain, is even more interesting because it is one of the more novelistic chapters of a life in which a love of science led our protagonist into a thousand dangerous, and exciting, adventures.

---

[7] Bread and Bulls. In Spanish in the original. (Tr. Note)

[8] The Homage Tower, whose dungeon was the crudest of prisons. In Spanish in the original. (Tr. Note)

CHAPTER THREE

harged by Napoleon with the task of measuring the meridian, M. Arago was in Majorca in 1808 on the mountain that is known as the *Esclop de Galatzo*[1], when word reached him of the events in Madrid, and the abduction of Ferdinand. The

---

[1] The three times that George Sand refers to this mountain, she calls it the Leclop de Galatzó, not the Clot as was mistakenly printed in the first edition of "Un Hiver a Majorque" (Hippolyte Souverain – Paris 1842), an error which was reproduced in all successive editions.

George Sand knew how to write *L'Esclop* in good Majorcan, but Leclop aided the reader's understanding that a mountain was being referred to, while *Clot* means an excavation, a hole.

We have established the truth after consulting the original manuscript in the Cell-Museum at the Carthusian monastery in Valldemosa. (Editor's Note).

exasperation of the inhabitants of Majorca was such that they, in some way, held the erudite Frenchman responsible, and headed, en masse, up the *Esclop de Galatzo* to kill him.

This mountain is situated on the coast from which James I descended to lead his successful conquest of Majorca from the Moors. As M. Arago often lit fires for his personal use, the Majorcans took these to be beacons, signalling to a squadron of French ships carrying troops ready to disembark.

One of these islanders, named Damian, the chief helmsman on a barque assigned by the Spanish government to help with the meridian project, resolved to warn Arago of the danger he faced. He ran ahead of his compatriots, and hurriedly took the Frenchman a sailor suit, with which to disguise himself.

Arago immediately left the mountain, and walked into Palma. Along the way he met the same gang who were planning to beat him to death and they asked him for any information he might have as to the whereabouts of the damned "gavatxo"[2] they planned to get rid of. As he spoke the language of the country well, M. Arago responded to all of their questions, and was not recognised.

On arriving in Palma, he went to his barque; but the captain, Don Manuel de Vacaro, who up to then had been at his command, formally refused to take him to

---

[2] A derogatory term used by the Spanish and Catalans to refer to the French. It is spelt "Gabacho" in Spanish. (Tr. Note)

Barcelona, and only offered him, in refuge, a wooden crate, into which M. Arago proved unable to fit.

The following morning, a threatening group had formed up along the shoreline, and Captain Vacaro warned M. Arago that from that moment forth, he would no longer be answerable for his life, adding that, in agreement with the opinion of the Capitan General, he considered that there was no other way to save his life, other than to surrender himself as a prisoner to the fort of Bellver. To facilitate this surrender, he was given a small boat, in which to cross the bay. The locals became aware of this, and launched themselves in pursuit. They were just about to capture him, when the doors of the fortress closed behind him.

M. Arago was in the prison for two months, until the Capitan General sent him word that he would turn a blind eye to any escape attempt he might make. He managed to get away with the help of Señor Rodriguez, his Spanish colleague on the meridian measurement project.

Damian, the same Majorcan who had saved his life on the *Esclop de Galtazo*, took him to Algeria in a fishing boat, not wishing to disembark in France, or Spain, for love, nor money.

During his captivity, M. Arago learned from some Swiss soldiers who were guarding him that some monks had offered them money to have him poisoned.

In Africa, our erudite hero had many misadventures, which he managed to survive even more miraculously; but I am straying from my subject here;

I can but hope that, one day, he himself will narrate this fascinating tale.

At first sight, the Majorcan capital does not reveal much of its character. Only by meandering around its interior, penetrating its arcane and mysterious streets of an evening, can one be surprised at the style, and elegance, or the astonishing disposition of even its minor edifices. However, it is the northern side, when approaching from the interior of the island, that the city reveals all of its African physiognomy.

M. Laurens felt this picturesque beauty, which might not have impressed a simple archaeologist, and he depicted one of the views that also impressed me, with its grandeur and melancholy; it is the part of the ramparts, not far from the church of Saint Augustine, where there is an enormous stretch of bare wall in which the only opening is a small arched door, crowned by a group of beautiful palm trees.

This is the last vestiges of a Templar fortress. It forms the foreground, admirable in its starkness and sadness, to the magnificent panorama that extends beyond the wall, where the cheerful and fertile plain disappears into the distant blue mountains of Valldemosa. Towards evening, the colour of the landscape varies from one hour to the next, producing a constantly evolving, harmonic effect. At sunset, we have seen a glorious pink become a splendid violet, changing to a silvery purple, and finally a pure and transparent blue, as night begins to fall.

M. Laurens has drawn many other views from the

vantage point of the walls of Palma.

"Each evening," he says, "at the hour in which the sun vividly colours everything, I would slowly wander over to the ramparts, continually stopping to contemplate the happy accidents that result from the arrangement of the lines of the mountains or the sea with the tops of the buildings of the city.

"Here the inner parapet of the walls is adorned with a formidable bush of aloes out of which grow hundreds of high stalks whose inflorescence unmistakably brings to mind a monumental candelabra. Then there are groups of palm trees that elevate themselves above the gardens where they grow among fig trees, cacti, orange trees and arborescent castor oil plants; further on appear terraces and panoramic viewing points under the shade of vines and finally the spires of the cathedral, the bell towers and the domes of numerous churches silhouetted against the pure and luminous background of the sky."

Another walk in which the sympathies of M. Laurens coincide with mine was among the ruins of Saint Dominic's monastery.

At the end of a canopy of vines held up by marble pillars, there are four huge palm trees, made to appear giant sized by the elevation of the garden in terraces, and which form a true part of the landscape of the city, since they are on the same level as the rooftops. Through their branches can be glimpsed the apex of the façade of Saint Stephen's, the massive tower with the celebrated Balearic clock[3], and the Angel tower of the Royal Palace.

This monastery of the inquisition, of which little remains now but a pile of ruins pierced here and there by bushes, and aromatic herbs, was not raised to the ground by the hand of time. It was a hand more purposeful, and more inexorable, that of revolution, which tore it down, and almost reduced it to dust a few years ago. It is said that it was a masterpiece, and, indeed, its vestiges - fragments of rich mosaic, some light arches still standing in the middle of the emptiness like skeletons- attest to its former magnificence.

The destruction of these sanctuaries of catholic art, across the whole of Spain, provokes great indignation

---

[3] This clock, which the two principal Majorcan historians, Dimeto and Mut described at great length, was still in use thirty years ago, as witness what M. Grasset de Saint-Sauveur had to say about it: "This ancient artefact is called the Sun Clock. It marks the hours between when the sun rises, and sets, matching the longer, or shorter, diurnal or nocturnal arc. On the 10th June, the first hour of the day it strikes, is half-past five, and the fourteenth, is half-past seven. The first hour of the night, is then half past eight, and the ninth hour is half past four, the following morning. From the 10th of December, it is the opposite. During the course of the entire year, the hours are exactly regulated, in accordance with the variations of sunrise and sunset. This clock is not of much use to the people of the country, who employ modern clocks, but gardeners still use it to determine the best time for watering. It is not known from where, or in what era, the clock was brought to Palma; it is not believed to have come from Spain, France, Germany, or Italy, where the Romans introduced the practise of dividing the day up into twelve hours, beginning at sunrise.

"Nevertheless, a churchman, who was the rector of the University of Palma, in the third part of a work on seraphic religion, affirms that some refugee Jews, at the time of Vespasian, took the famous clock from the ruins of Jerusalem, and transported it to Majorca, to whence they had fled. This marvellous origin, would appeal to the inclination towards the prodigious, which characterises our islanders.

"The historian Dameto, and his disciple Mut, could only trace the clock back as far as 1385, when it was bought by some Dominican fathers, and placed in the tower where it is still found." (*Voyage to the Balearics and Pitiusas*, 1807). [Author's Note].

among the Palman aristocracy, and is a source of justified lamentation among artists. Perhaps ten years ago, I too would have been more shocked by the vandalism of this destruction than by the page of history it illustrates.

However, even though it is possible to deplore, as Marliani does in his *Political History of Modern Spain*, the wretched and violent side of the measures which that decree led to, I must confess that among those ruins, I felt an emotion that was not the sadness that such ruins ordinarily inspire. Lightning had struck there, and lightning is a blind tool, a brutal force like the ire of man; nevertheless, the laws of Providence which govern the elements and preside over apparent chaos know very well that beneath the ashes of ruins are hidden the beginnings of a new life. The day the monasteries fell, the political atmosphere of Spain experienced something analogous to the need for renovation that nature undergoes in its fecund convulsions.

I do not accept what I heard in Palma, that it was a few malcontents avid for vengeance, or loot, that carried out that act of violence against the wishes of a dismayed public. There must have been a great many malcontents, to have reduced such an enormous mass of buildings to rubble, and there must have been very little sympathy among the general public, if they just stood by while the decree was carried out against their heartfelt protests.

I believe, rather, that the first stone torn out of the top of those domes brought down with it a sense of fear and respect, which had oppressed the soul of the people, and that had been sustained as weakly as the monastic bell tower on its foundations. I think that, suddenly, and mysteriously, one and all experienced a sudden, and deeply felt, impulse to leap upon the cadaver with a mixture of courage and dread, fury and remorse. Monasticism sheltered many abuses, and bolstered many egos; but devoutness is very strong in Spain, and without doubt more than one of the demolishers felt remorse for their action, and rushed to confession the following day to the priest who they had just jettisoned from his refuge. However, even in the heart of the most blind and ignorant man, there is something that makes him tremble with enthusiasm when destiny confers on him a sovereign mission.

The Spanish people had built those insolent palaces of the regular clergy with their money, and their sweat, at whose doors people had queued for centuries to receive a morsel of loafer's charity, or the bread of intellectual slavery. They had participated in the church's crimes, and had been steeped in its cowardliness. They had built the bonfires of the Inquisition. They had been accomplices, and informers, in atrocious persecutions aimed at entire races that they wished to extirpate from their midst. Then, once they had completed the ruin of the Jews who had enriched them, once they had driven out the Moors, to whom they owed their civilisation and grandeur, they suffered, as if by heavenly retribution, misery and ignorance. Still, they had the tenacity, and the piety not to blame it on these clergy, their creation,

116

their corruptor and their scourge. They suffered for a long time, bent under that yoke they had fashioned with their own hands. Then one day, some strange, audacious voices whispered words of emancipation and deliverance into their ears and consciences. Then they understood the mistakes of their ancestors, they were embarrassed at their abasement, indignant at their misery and, despite the veneration that they still retained towards images and relics, they broke these idols up, and began to believe more forcefully in their own rights, than in their religion.

What secret force could suddenly cause a prostrated devotee to rise up, and direct his fanaticism, even if only for one day, against the objects he had adored all his life? It surely was not mere discontent with men, or disgust at things. It was indubitably self-loathing, repugnance at their own timidity.

The Spanish people showed a greatness that day of which we had not thought them capable. They acted decisively, and cut off all means at their disposal which would allow them to retreat from their determination, like a boy who desires to be a man, and so breaks all of his toys to ensure he cannot be further tempted to play with them.

As for Don Juan Mendizabal (when speaking of these events it is most fitting to mention his name), if what I have learned of his political career has been faithfully recounted to me, he must be more a man of principle, than a man of action, and for me, that is the best eulogy that can be dedicated to him. This man of state overestimated, at a certain time, the intellectual situation in Spain, and in yet another he underestimated it, at times he took inopportune or incomplete measures and sowed his ideas on barren ground, where the seed was choked, or devoured. This should perhaps be reason enough to deny him the skill of execution, and persistence of character that immediate success demands of its enterprises; but it is not enough for history, considered from the most philosophic point of view, from which it is rarely viewed, to deny him his place as one of the most generous, and ardently progressive, spirits in Spain.[4]

---

[4] This rectitude of ideas, and this elevated sense of history, inspired M. Marliani when he was writing a eulogy on Mendizabal for the opening pages of a critique of his ministry: "...There are admirable qualities that one can never deny him, qualities that were rare in the men who proceeded him to power: faith in the future of his country, a limitless dedication to the cause of liberty, a passionate sense of nationality, a sincere enthusiasm for progressive, and even revolutionary, ideas necessary to bring about the reforms the Spanish state needed; great tolerance, great generosity towards his enemies; in short, a personal disinterest that in every moment, and on every occasion, caused him to sacrifice his own interests for those of his country, and which led him to leave several ministries, without even a medal to show for his trouble... He was the first prime minister to take the regeneration of his country seriously. His time in government represented a real step forward. The minister, then, spoke the language of the patriot. He did not have enough power to abolish censorship, but he had the generosity to free the press of any hindrance, even when this benefited his enemies, more than himself. He submitted his administrative acts to the free scrutiny of public opinion, and when a violent opposition to him was fostered in parliament, by former friends, he had enough stateliness to respect the freedom of the minister, within the bureaucratic hierarchy. He declared in parliament that he would rather cut off his hand, than sign the dismissal of a minister who had once benefited from his favours and who had now become his most ardent political enemy. Mendizabal provided a noble example, and a meritorious one, since he had no comparable model to follow! After him, no disciple of this virtuous tolerance has been found. (*A Political History of Modern Spain*, by Marliani). [Author's note].

Interior of the Carthusian
(Drawing by Parcerisa)

Valldemosa – Cemetery
(drawing by Laurens)

These reflections came to me often among the ruins of the monasteries of Majorca. When I heard people curse his name, I knew it was perhaps inconvenient for us to defend him in a tone of approval and empathy; but I told myself then, that beyond the political questions of the day, which I can say that I neither liked nor understood, there was a synthetic judgement that I could apply to men, and even to deeds, without fear of deceiving myself. In order to get an accurate idea of a nation, and to conceive the true sense of its history, its future and its moral life, it is not as essential as many believe, and say, to directly get to know a nation, or to have studied its customs and its material life. It appears to me, that in the general history of human life, there is a great line to follow that is the same for all peoples, and to which all the threads of individual histories are connected. This line is the perpetual feeling for, and effort towards, the ideal, or if you prefer, perfectibility, which all men bear within them, whether in a state of blind instinct, or enlightened theory. Really eminent men have felt it, and have all practiced it, more or less in their own way, and the most daring, those who have had the most lucid revelation and have given the greatest impulses in the present to hasten the development of the future, are those whose contemporaries have nearly always adjudged them worst. They have been stigmatised, and condemned, often by people who did not know the least thing about them, and they were not allowed back onto the pedestal from which they had been cast down by some fleeting disappointment, or some misapprehended setback, until much later, when the fruit of their labours had been harvested.

How many famous names from our revolution were rehabilitated too late, and with reticence! How many of them are there whose mission is still misunderstood, and poorly developed? In Spain, Mendizabal was one of the most severely judged ministers, because he was the most courageous, perhaps the only one to be so; and the act that marks his brief tenure in power with an ineffaceable memory, the radical destruction of the monasteries, has been portrayed in such a bad light, that I feel the need to protest here, in favour of that audacious resolution, and the intoxication with which the Spanish people adopted it, and carried it out.

This, at least, is the feeling that suddenly filled my soul on observing those ruins, that time has still not blackened, and which also seem to protest against the past, and proclaim the awakening of the truth in the people. I do not feel that I have lost my respect for, or taste in, the arts, and I have no instincts for vengeance, or barbarism; in short, I am not one of those who say that the cult of beauty is useless, and who demand that historical monuments should be degraded by making them into factories; nevertheless, a monastery of the Inquisition, torn to the ground by the arm of the people, represents a great page in history, a page as instructive, and emotive, as a Roman aqueduct, or an amphitheatre. A government office that orders the cold blooded destruction of a place of worship, for reasons of petty utility, or as part of some ridiculous economy drive, would be committing a crass, outrageous act. Notwithstanding, a political leader who, on a decisive and precarious day, sacrifices art and science for more precious gains, reason, justice, religious freedom, and a people who, despite their pious instincts, their love for the pomp of Catholicism, and their respect for its holy men, finds enough courage, and strength, to carry out that decree in a blink of an eye, do only what a crew of a ship at sea do when threatened by a storm, they throw overboard their treasures, in order to save their lives.

Let those who wish to cry over these ruins do so! Nearly all of the historical monuments whose fall we lament were prisons, where the human soul, or body, languished for centuries. Let poets come who, instead of bewailing the loss of innocence in the world, stand on the debris of these bloody rods and golden playthings to celebrate, in their verses, the virile age that grasps how to liberate us from them! There are some beautiful verses by Chamiso concerning the castle of his ancestors, torn down by the French Revolution. This piece ends with an idea new to both poetry, and politics:

Blessed are you, old manor, over which the ploughshare now passes!

And blessed be him who drives the plough over you!

After having evoked the memory of this beautiful poem, dare I transcribe some pages that the Dominican monastery inspired in me? Why not? Why should the reader not be tolerant towards some reflections that the author submits to him, written by sacrificing self-esteem, and my habitual tendencies. Whatever the outcome, this fragment will add some variety to the dry list of names of building I have just drawn up.

CHAPTER FOUR

THE MONASTERY OF THE INQUISITION

wo men met among the debris of a ruined monastery, beneath the serene clarity of moonlight. One seemed to be in the prime of life, the other bent nearly double with the weight of years, although, in fact this latter was the younger of the two.

The night was well advanced, and the streets deserted, when they met face to face, and they shivered as they heard the bell tower of the cathedral slowly, and lugubriously, toll the hour.

The one who appeared older was the first to speak:

"Whoever you are my man," he said, "have no fear of me; I am feeble and crooked: don't expect anything off me either, I am poor, and stripped of everything on this earth."

"My friend," responded the younger man, "I am only hostile to those who attack me, and, like you, I am too poor to fear thieves."

"Brother," continued the more withered of the pair, "why did you start so at my approach?"

"Because I am a little superstitious, like all artists, and I took you for the ghost of one of the monks that used to inhabit this place, the men on whose broken tombs we tread. And you friend, why did you shudder as you approached me?"

"Because I am very superstitious, like all monks, and I took you for the ghost of one of the monks who once buried me alive in the tombs, on which you are standing."

"What is that you say? Then you are one of the men I have been avidly, and vainly, searching for throughout Spain!"

"You will not find any of us by the light of the sun; but, in the shadows of the night, you may find us still. But now your wait is over, what do you want of a monk?"

"To look at you, and to ask you questions, Father; to fix all the details of your appearance in my mind, so that I can reproduce them later in painting; to collect your words, that I might repeat them to my compatriots; in short, to get to know you in order to penetrate what is mysterious, poetic, and exalted in the person of a monk, and in the life of the cloister."

"From where did you get these strange ideas, O Traveller? Are you not from a country where the Pope holds no sway, a country that has outlawed monks, and suppressed the cloisters?"

"Among us there are still souls who reverence the past; and ardent imaginations consumed by the poetry of the Middle Ages. We seek out anything that could give us even a whiff of that time, and we venerate it, indeed, almost adore it. Oh, do not think, Father, that we are all blind profaners. We artists hate the brutal mob, who soil and break everything they touch. Far from ratifying their sentences of death and destruction, we make an effort, in our paintings, our poetry, our plays, in fact, in all our works, to revive the old traditions, and to reanimate the spirit of mysticism that engendered Christian art, that sublime progeny!"

"What's that you say, my son? How can the artists of your flourishing and free country be inspired by anything, other than the present? There are so many new things to sing about, paint, or illustrate! Do they really live, as you say, attached to the land in which their ancestors sleep? Do they really rummage through the dust of tombs, in search of some radiant and fertile inspiration, when God, in His Goodness, has given them a life so sweet, and beautiful?"

"Ah, Father, I do not know what there is in our lives that you think so worthy. We artists do not concern ourselves in any way with politics; while social questions interest us even less. In vain, do we seek the poetry of that which surrounds us. The arts languish, inspiration is suffocated, bad taste is triumphant, and materialism absorbs men's interest. If it were not for the cult of the past, and the historical monuments of a time of faith to stimulate us, we would completely lose the sacred fire, which we so zealously guard."

"Be that as it may, I have been told that human genius has never achieved so much as in your land of science, of happiness. What of the marvels of industry, and the benefits of liberty? Have I been ill-informed?"

"If they told you, Father, that no other age has ever produced such welfare, and such great luxury, from its material riches, or salvaged such a horrendous mishmash of tastes, opinions, and beliefs out of the ruins of the former society, then you have been told the truth. But if they did not tell you that all of these things, instead of making us happy, have debased and degraded us, then they have not told you the whole truth."

"How has such a strange state of affairs come about? Have all the sources of happiness been poisoned on your lips? Have welfare and liberty, the things that make man great, and just and good, really made you insignificant and wretched? Explain this extraordinary phenomenon to me!"

"Well, Father, must I remind you that man shall not live by bread alone? If we have lost our faith, every other benefit we have acquired cannot feed our souls."

"Explain to me also, my son, how you have lost your

faith? If religious persecution has ceased among you, why have you not been able to open up your souls and lift your eyes to the Divine Light? This was the moment to believe, because this was the moment of knowledge! Did you really doubt in that moment? What cloud passed before your eyes then?"

"The cloud of weakness, and human misery. Are not research and faith two incompatibles, Father?"

"Ah, young man, that is like asking me if faith is compatible with truth. Do you not believe in anything, my son? Or do you believe in falsehood?"

"Alas, I do not believe in anything, except art. But is that not enough to give strength, confidence, and sublime joy to the soul?"

"I know not, my son. I still do not understand. Is there anyone left among you then who is happy? And you? Have you remained aloof from the despondency and anguish?"

"No Father, artists are the most wretched, the most indignant, the most tormented of men; for every day, they see the object of their worship brought further down, and their strength is not enough to raise it up again."

"How can men so perceptive let the arts perish, instead of reviving them?"

"They no longer have any faith, and without faith, art is impossible!"

"Have you not just told me that for you art is a religion? You contradict yourself, my son, or perhaps I do not fully understand you."

"How could we not be in contradiction with ourselves, we, who have received a mission from God that the world denies us; we, who see the doors of glory, inspiration, and life itself shut in our faces by the present-day; we, who are forced to live in the past, and to ask the dead for the secrets of an eternal beauty, whose tenets our contemporaries have rejected, whose altars they have lain waste? Before the works of the great masters, and when the hope of equalling their achievement is upon us, then are we full of strength and enthusiasm; but when we have to bring our ambitious dreams to fruition, and an incredulous and narrow minded world blows the icy winds of disdain and scorn in our faces, then we can achieve nothing that comes close to our ideal, and the insight dies in our breast, without ever seeing the light of day."

The young artist spoke with bitterness, the moon illuminating his sad, proud face, and the motionless monk contemplated him with benevolent, and naive surprise.

"Let us sit here," said the latter, after a moment's silence, stopping alongside the solid railing of a terrace which overlooked the city, the fields, and the sea.

They were in that section of the Dominicans' garden that, until recently, abounded in flowers, fountains and precious marbles, but that today is sown with rubble, and invaded by a confusion of long weeds that grow among the ruins with such speed and vigour.

The traveller, in his agitation, tore one up with his bare hand, and, with a sudden cry of pain, threw it far from him. The monk smiled.

La Granja (Esporlas)
(drawing by Furió)

The Carthusian Manastery at Valldemossa
(drawing by Parcerisa)

"That weed pricks," he said. "But it is not dangerous. Oh my child, that thorn you carelessly handled, and that has hurt you, is symbolic of those vulgar men who you have been railing against. They have invaded the palaces and monasteries. They creep up the altars, and cling to the remains of the antique splendours of this world. Look at the vitality and strength with which these weeds have invaded the parterres, where we carefully raised delicate and valued plants, not one of which has been able to resist our desertion. In the same way, the simple and half savage men who were formerly thrown out like useless weeds, have now recovered their rights, and smothered the poisonous plant growing in the shadows, that was known as the Inquisition."

"Could they not have smothered it without destroying the sanctuaries of Christian art, and the works of genius?"

"It was necessary to root out this noxious plant, because it was active, and creeping everywhere. They had to destroy even the foundations on which this monastery was built, to get at its deepest roots."

"Then tell me Father, these thorny weeds that are growing in its stead, in what way are they beautiful, and in what way are they beneficial?"

The monk thought for a moment, and then replied:

"You say you are a painter. Do you plan to make a drawing of these ruins?"

"Indeed. But where is this leading?"

"Will you leave out these great clumps of weed that festoon the ruins, and sway in the breeze? Or will you make them the happy accessories of your composition, as I have seen in a painting by Salvatore Rosa?"

"They are the inseparable companions of these ruins, and every painter should take advantage of them."

"So they do have their beauty then, their meaning, and therefore their use."

"Your parable is not fair, Father; if Gypsies and Bohemians were to sit on these rocks, they would only appear more desolate, and sinister. The painting would gain thereby, but what would humanity gain?"

"Perhaps a beautiful painting, and surely a great lesson. But you artists, who give this lesson, do not understand what you do, and only see here some fallen rocks, and weeds growing."

"You are harsh. Hearing you speak thus, I could reply that you do not see anything more in this catastrophe than the destruction of your prison, and the recovery of your freedom, because I begin to suspect that the monastery was not to your liking Father."

"And you my son, do you love art and poetry so much, that you could live here without regret?"

"I imagine that, for me, this would have been the most beautiful life in the world! Oh, how vast this monastery must have been, and what a noble style it must have displayed! What splendour and elegance are proclaimed by these remains! How sweet it must have been to come here at eventide, to breathe the dulcet breeze, and meditate on the sound of the sea, when these airy galleries were paved with rich mosaics, and crystalline

waters murmured within marble basins, and a silver
lamp had been lit, like some faint star, in the depths of
the sanctuary! What profound peace, what majestic
silence you must have enjoyed, when the confidence and
respect of your fellow men formed an invincible barrier
around you, and people crossed themselves, and lowered
their voices, whenever they passed your mysterious
portals! Ah, who would not have wanted to abjure all
preoccupations, all hardship, and all ambition of social
life, to bury themselves here, in tranquillity, forgotten by
the outside world, yet, to remain an artist, and to be able
to devote ten or twenty years to a single work of art, that
you could refine slowly, polishing it like a precious
diamond, and that would be placed above an altar, not to
be judged and criticised by the first ignoramus that saw
it, but rather to be acknowledged, and invoked as an
admirable representation of Divinity itself!"

"Outsider," said the monk in a stern tone, "...your
words are full of pride, and your dreams are mere
vanity. In this art, of which you speak with such
emphasis and esteem, you see nothing but yourself, and
the isolation you wish for would only be a means for you
to aggrandise and deify yourself! Now I understand how
you can believe in this narcissistic art without believing
in any religion, or society. Perhaps you have not given
mature consideration to these things before opening your
mouth about them; perhaps you are unaware of what
really went on in these dens of corruption and terror.
Come with me, perhaps what I am about to show you will

change your mind, and your feelings about this place."

The monk led him, not without peril, through heaps of rubble, past crumbling and precarious precipices, and into the heart of the ruined monastery to where the dungeons had been. Here he made him carefully descend past a long bare wall, fifteen foot thick, that picks and shovels had now shattered. In the hub of this petrifying bulwark of stone and cement, there were revealed dark, airless cells, now like open mouths gaping out of the earth, each one separated from its neighbour by walls as thick as those which suspended weightily over their dismal vaults.

"Young man," said the monk. "These pits, that you can see are not wells, they are not even tombs; they are the cells of the Inquisition. For centuries, it was here that men languished, and perished, whether they were guilty or innocent in the eyes of God. Degraded by vice, or deluded by rage, inspired by genius, or by virtue, they died, because they dared to hold opinions different to those of the Inquisition.

"These Dominican Fathers were wise, educated, even artists. They had extensive libraries, in which the subtleties of theology, leather bound and decorated in gold, were exhibited on shelves of ebony, whose edges shone with pearls and rubies. Nevertheless, Man, that Living Book into which God had written His thoughts with His own Hand, was made to descend into the entrails of the earth, to be kept locked up there. They had cups of chiselled silver, magnificent chalices resplendent in precious stones, wonderful paintings, and sculpted Virgins in gold and ivory; and yet they took Man, that chosen chalice of Celestial Grace, that Living Image of God Himself, and abandoned him, still breathing, among the worms, and the stony cold of the tomb. One of them cultivated roses and jonquils, with the same care and love with which you would rear a child, yet he watched with indifference as his fellow man, his brother, was left to pale, and rot, in the dank of the sepulchre.

"That is what it meant to be a monk, my son. That was the reality of the cloister. On the one hand, ferocious brutality, terror and cowardice; and on the other, egotistical intellect, or callous devotion; that is what the Inquisition represented.

"And if the liberators who opened these rank dungeons to the light came upon some gilded columns, that they tore down and stripped; would you have had them put the tombstone back on top of those dying victims, and shed tears for their executioners, because they were about to lose some gold, and some slaves?"

Curiosity had led the artist to descend into one of the pits to examine the walls. For an instant, he tried to imagine the struggle of human will, buried alive, to sustain life against the awful desperation of such captivity. But barely had he painted that picture in his quick and fertile imagination, than he felt a tremble of anxiety, and terror. He believed he sensed the icy vaults above him weighing down on his soul, and he gasped for air in his lungs. Feeling as if he were about to faint, he wished to leap out of that terrible abyss, without delay. Stretching out his arms towards the monk, who had remained in the entranceway, he cried out:

"Help me Father! In the Name of God help me get out of here!"

"Ah, my child," said the monk offering him his hand. "What do you feel now, when you see the stars shining above your head? Well, imagine how I felt when I saw the sun again, after ten years of such torment!"

"Unhappy monk!" exclaimed the traveller, hastening their pace towards the garden; were you able to stand ten years of this premature death, without losing your reason or your life? I think if I had stayed there a moment longer, I would surely have turned witless or raving mad. No, I would not have believed that the sight of a dungeon could produce such sudden, such profound terrors, and I cannot understand how one could ever accustom oneself to them. I have seen instruments of torture in Venice; I have also seen the dungeons of the Duke's palace, and the blind alley, where victims were struck down by unseen hands, and the holes in the tiles, through which the blood flowed, and ran off into the canals, without a trace. There the idea was a more or less swift death. But in this Inferno we have just been in, what comes to my mind is the terrifying thought of being alive there! Oh dear God! To be there, and unable to die!"

"Look at me, my son," said the monk, revealing his bald and emaciated head; "I am no older in years than you. Yet, with your vigorous face and serene look, I am sure that you took me for an old man.

"It is not important what I did to deserve my slow agony, nor how I survived it. I am not asking for your pity; nor do I need it. Looking at these ruined walls and these empty dungeons, I feel as happy, and youthful, as I could be. Nor do I wish to inspire in you a hate towards the monks, they are free, as I am free now. God is good to everyone. However, as you are an artist, it would be good if you understood these emotions, without which the artist cannot comprehend his work.

"Now, if you wish to paint these ruins, to which you came a short while ago to weep over a lost past, and among which I come every night to prostrate myself, and give thanks to God for the present, perhaps your hand will now be inspired by higher thoughts than a cowardly nostalgia, or a sterile admiration for the past. Many historical monuments that are objects of infinite value for historians have no other merit that that of reminding us what humanity achieved in building them, and that was often something iniquitous or puerile. As you have travelled, perhaps you have seen, in Genoa, a bridge with gargantuan piers, suspended over an abyss, and on the other side an opulent and substantial church, built in a deserted area by a rich aristocrat because, in his vanity, he did not wish to kneel in a church besides the adherents of his parish, nor cross the water to pray elsewhere. Perhaps you have also seen the Pyramids of Egypt, those horrifying testaments to the slavery of nations, or those dolmens, over whose stones flowed torrents of human blood to satisfy the inexhaustible thirst of the Barbarian gods. But the majority of you artists only see in the works of man the beauty or singularity of their construction, without troubling yourselves about the idea of which the building is the physical manifestation. So, your intellect usually adores the expression of a sentiment which your heart would reject, if it was conscious of it.

"That is why your works often lack the true colours of life, above all when, instead of expressing the life that flows through the veins of humanity, you force yourselves to coldly interpret the lives of the dead, that you cannot even understand."

"Father," responded the young man. "I understand your lessons, and I do not reject everything you say; but do you believe that art can truly be inspired by such philosophies? You try to explain, using the reason of our age, that which was conceived in the poetic delirium of our superstitious ancestors. If instead of the smiling deities of Greece, we were to strip bare the banal allegories that lie behind their voluptuous forms; if instead of the divine Madonna of the Florentines, we were to paint a full-bodied serving wench, like the Dutch do; in short, if we were to make Jesus, the Son of God, into a naive philosopher of the Platonic school, then instead of divinities, we would have nothing more than mortal men, just like here, instead of a Christian temple, we now have nothing more than a pile of stones."

"My son," replied the monk. "If the Florentines managed to give divine features to the Virgin, it was because they still believed in Her. If the Dutch gave Her coarse features, it was because they no longer believed in Her. And you artists who pride yourselves today on painting sacred themes, you who do not even believe in anything but art, in other words, in nothing but yourselves! You will never achieve anything! You should not try to escape into the past, but rather only reproduce that which is palpable and alive today!

"If I were a painter, I would have painted a beautiful painting illustrating the day of my liberation; it would have depicted valiant and hearty men, with a hammer in one hand and a torch in the other, penetrating these Purgatories of the Inquisition that I have just shown you, and lifting ghosts, with blinking eyes and frightened smiles, out from beneath those fetid flagstones. There would have been light from the sky, shafting down through the broken vaults, and illuminating their heads like haloes. It would have been a beautiful subject, as appropriate for my time as the Last Judgement was for Michelangelo; because these men from the village, who seem to you so vulgar and coarse in their orgy of destruction, seem more noble and beautiful than all the angels of heaven to me; just as this ruin, which for you is an object of sadness and consternation, is, for me, a more religious monument now than it ever was before its fall.

"If I were in charge of raising an altar designed to transmit to future ages the greatness and strength of our age, I would not wish for better than this pile of stones, above which I would place a consecrated commemorative inscription saying:

"In a time of ignorance and cruelty, men worshipped on this altar a God of vengeance and torture. On the day of justice and in the name of humanity, men tore down these bloody altars as abominations before the God of mercy."

CHAPTER FIVE

I t was not in Palma, but in Barcelona, in the ruins of the House of the Inquisition, where I saw the deeply dug dungeons with their fifteen foot thick walls. It is quite possible that there were, in fact, no prisoners to be liberated in that of Palma when it was torn down. It is only right that I ask the susceptible Majorcans to pardon me for my poetic licence in the chapter you have just read.

Nevertheless, I would like to point out that nothing is invented that does not have a certain basis in fact. In Majorca I met a priest, who is today the rector of a parish in Palma, who told me that he had spent seven years of his life "the flower of his youth" in Inquisition prisons, and that he had only been freed thanks to the influence of a lady who had taken a great interest in him. He was a man in his prime, with animated eyes and a jovial manner. He did not appear to feel much sorrow at the demise of the Holy Office.

As for the Dominican monastery, let me quote a passage from M. Grasset de Saint-Sauveur, who no-one would accuse of partiality, since he had previously pompously eulogised the Inquisitors who he had met on Majorca.

"However, in Saint Dominic's monastery, one can still see pictures that prompt memories of the barbaric acts of violence to which the Jews were subjected. Each of these unfortunates is represented in a picture, at whose foot appears their name, age, and the date on which they were burned at the stake.

"I am assured that a few years ago, the descendents of those unfortunates, who today form a particular sub-class given the ridiculous name of the *Jewettes*[1], had vainly offered quite large sums to get these upsetting reminders removed. I however, do not believe this story...

"I will never forget, however, one particular day, when I was wandering around the Dominican monastery, gazing sorrowfully on these cheerless pictures: a monk approached me, and pointed out to me that many of the

---

[1] Note: the original has *chouettes*, which in French could imply a certain type of owl, leading the author to view it as a ridiculous nickname. However, this ornithological co-incidence is not present in Catalan, where the word she heard: "Xuetes" is a term derived from the word for Jews. [Tr. Note].

paintings were marked with crossed bones. He told me that they were the portraits of those whose ashes were scattered to the four winds.

"My blood ran cold, and I left forthwith, my heart full sore, and my soul in anguish.

"Quite by chance I stumbled upon a report, printed in 1755, on the orders of the Inquisition, with the names, surnames, occupations, and charges brought against those sentenced on Majorca from 1645 to 1691.

"I shuddered as I read that document: I found four Majorcans, a woman amongst them, burned alive, accused of practicing Judaism; another thirty-two, accused of the same offence, died in the Inquisition's cells and their bodies were burned; three whose ashes were exhumed and thrown to the winds; a Dutchman accused of Lutheranism, a Majorcan of Mohammedanism; six Portuguese, a woman among them, and seven Majorcans accused of Judaism - they were lucky to escape, and so they were merely burned in effigy. There were another two hundred and sixteen victims, Majorcans and foreigners, accused of Judaism, Mohammedanism or heresy, who managed to leave the prisons, after having publicly recanted, and being taken back into the bosom of the Church.

"This horrifying catalogue concluded with a decree issued by the inquisition that was no less horrifying."

M. Grasset then quotes the Spanish text, of which I offer a faithful translation:

"All of the prisoners contained in this report have been condemned publicly by the Holy Office as formal heretics; all of their goods have been confiscated and donated to the Royal Treasury. They have been declared incompetent and barred from obtaining or holding or acceding to any positions or benefits, whether ecclesiastical or secular, or holding public office, whether honorary or bona fide. Neither they nor their dependants are to be permitted to carry on their persons gold, silver, pearls, gemstones, coral, silk, camlet or fine cloth; nor may they ride horses or carry arms, nor may they exercise or use other items that, by common law, the laws and sanctions of the Kingdom, or the instructions or regulations of the Holy Office, are denied to persons thus classified. For females condemned to the flames, the same prohibition extends to their sons and their daughters and for men, to their grandchildren of the male line. Also condemned are the memory and reputation of those executed in effigy. It is herby ordained that their bones (where they can be distinguished from those of the Christian faithful) shall be exhumed, delivered unto the judiciary and the secular authorities and thereby burned and reduced to ashes. All inscriptions found on the tombs of these heretics shall be effaced or rubbed away, whether these be found fastened or painted onto the sepulchres or on coats of arms. This should be carried out in such a way as to ensure that *no trace of them remains on the face of the earth except for the record of their sentence and execution.*"

When one reads documents like these, so close in time to our own era, and when one glimpses such invincible hate towards the descendents of these converted Jews on Majorca, even after twelve or fifteen generations, I cannot accept that the spirit of the Inquisition has been as entirely extinguished as people say it has since the time of Mendizabal's decree.

I will not finish this article, nor leave behind the Monastery of the Inquisition, without telling my readers of a curious discovery, the credit for which belongs entirely to M. Tastu, and which, thirty years ago, would have made the fortune of this erudite gentleman, unless, with a happy heart, he was willing to offer it to the Lord of the World[2] without craving any benefit out of it for himself, a supposition that corresponds more to his character as a disinterested and carefree artist than the other.

The note is too interesting for me to abridge it. Here it is then, exactly as it came into my hands, with the authorization to publish it.

SAINT DOMINIC'S MONASTERY
IN PALMA, MAJORCA

Miguel de Fabra, a companion of Saint Dominic, was the founder of the order of evangelical brothers on Majorca. He was originally from Old Castile and accompanied James I during the conquest of the Balearic Major in 1229. He was a widely educated man of notable piety, which gave him considerable authority with *The*

---

[2] The author is referring to Napoleon here. (Tr. Note)

Conqueror, his nobles, companions and even amongst the foot soldiers. He harangued the troops, officiated at mass, dispensed Holy Communion, and fought the infidel, as churchmen did in that age. The Moors claimed that only the Blessed Virgin and Father Miguel had really conquered them. The Aragonese and Catalan soldiers were said to pray to God and the Blessed Virgin; and then to Father Miguel Fabra.

The illustrious Dominican had taken the habit of his order in Toulouse from the hands of his friend Dominic, who sent him to Paris, along with two other companions, to fulfil a very important mission. It was he who established the first Dominican monastery in Palma, thanks to a donation that was given by J.R. de Torella, the procurator of the first Bishop of Majorca, all of which happened in 1231.

A mosque, and a few patches of land pertaining to it, served as the first foundation. The evangelical brothers would later expand the community, through lucrative trade in all kinds of goods, and through donations, which the faithful regularly gave. However, Brother Miguel de Fabra[3], the first founder, then left for Valencia, which he had helped conquer, to die.

The architect of the Dominican Monastery was Jaume Fabra. It is not known if he was of the same family as Father Miguel, whose surname he shared; we only know

---

[3] The author writes "frere de" – *the brother of* – here. However, as Miguel de Fabra has been established as the founder from the opening sentence of this section, it appears to me obvious that either George Sand was hasty in her copying, or M. Tastu made a mistake here that George Sand faithfully reproduces. (Tr. Note)

that he delivered the plans around 1296, and that later he drew up the drafts for Barcelona Cathedral (1317), and many other buildings in the lands under the Aragon Crown.

Judging by their appearance, the monastery and its church must have undergone many changes over time, if we compare, for a moment, as we have done, the different parts of the ruined buildings. Still standing, but only just, is a splendid portal echoing the style of the 14th century; but beyond it, and forming part of the building, are those broken arches, those heavy keystones from vaults that lie among the rubble, proving that many architects spent time here, but that they were all inferior to Jaume de Fabra.

Among these extensive ruins, of which little remain standing other than a few centenary palm trees, preserved thanks to our insistent supplication, we have deplored, (as we have in Saint Catherine's and Saint Francis' in Barcelona), that only the cold hand of politicians presided over these indiscriminating demolitions.

In fact, art and history have lost little with the destruction of Saint Jerome's in Palma, or the Monastery of Saint Francis, which bordered and obstructed the sea wall at Barcelona; but in the name of History and Art, why did they not preserve, as historical monuments, the monasteries of Saint Catherine in Barcelona, and Saint Dominic in Palma, whose naves housed *les sepultres de persones de bé*[4] (the tombs of decent people) as is stated in a little notebook which passed through our hands, and

---

[4] The original is in a curious mixture of Spanish and Catalan. It is unclear whether this was an error in the original, the copy made by Tastu, or by Sand herself. In utilizing this quote, I have preferred the standard Catalan used in Majorca today. (Tr. Note)

which formed part of the monastery archives? Within its pages, one reads the name of N. Cotoner, Grand Master of Malta, as well as the Dameto, Muntaner, Villalonga, La Romana and *Bonapart* families! This book, like everything else in the monastery, now belongs to the demolition crews.

A typical Majorcan, who on first impression alarmed us, but later on calmed and captivated us, when he saw the interest that we took in those historical ruins (and besides, like all men of the people, he was an admirer of the Great Napoleon), hastened to point out to us the tomb with the coat of arms of the *Bonapart* family, his ancestors, if you accept Majorcan tradition. We found this interesting enough to merit further study, but we were so occupied with other work, that we were unable to find the time, or the attention, needed to research further.

We have, however, found the coat of arms of the *Bonapart* family, which we hereafter describe:

A shield divided into three parts. The single upper section being gold coloured, and showing an eagle rising. The lower section further divided into two parts, with a blue part, and a red part. On the left-hand section, are three pairs of six pointed, golden stars. On the right-hand section is a golden lion, walking on his hind legs.

We have made copies of some shields we found in a book on heraldry, which formed part of the riches of the library of the Count of Montenegro.

In Barcelona, we consulted another Spanish book of heraldry, not as beautifully crafted as the former, belonging to the erudite archivist of the Crown of

Aragon. Dated 15th June 1594, in this book can be found the evidence of the noble nature of the Fortuny family, among their four coats of arms, mounted on a shield, figures that of the maternal grandmother, who was from the house of *Bonapart*.

In the register: Index: Peter III, volume II, of the archives of the Crown of Aragon, two acts, dated 1276, are mentioned, referring to the *Bonpar* family. This name, originating in Provence, or the Languedoc area, has obviously undergone alterations in Majorca, like so many others, and become Bonapart.

In 1411, Hugo Bonapart, a native of Majorca, went to Corsica as regent, or governor, for King Martin of Aragon, and it is through him that the name Bonaparte, or later Buonaparte, arrived on that island. Thus, Bonapart is a Romance name, Bonaparte is Old Italian, and Buonaparte is modern Italian. It is known that the members of Napoleon's family signed themselves Bonaparte, or Buonaparte, indiscriminately.

Who knows what importance this slight evidence might have had a few years ago, if they could have been used to demonstrate to Napoleon, who wanted so badly to be French, that his ancestors were indeed Frenchmen?

M. Tastu's discovery is still interesting today, even if it does not have the same political importance it would have had not long ago. If I had sway over the purse strings of the department of the French Government who finance the Arts, I would ensure that M. Tastu was given the means to complete his research.

The French origins of Napoleon matter little today, I concur. That great Captain, who in my opinion (and I apologise for being unfashionable) was no great prince, but obviously a great man who has been unreservedly adopted by France. Posterity will probably not question if his ancestors were Florentines, Corsicans, Majorcans, or from the Languedoc area; but with history, it is always interesting to lift the veil that covered the predestination of this family, for which Napoleon appears not to have been such a fortuitous accident, or an isolated incident. I am sure that if his roots were to be traced, then examples would be found in the family of men, and women, who were worthy of such a descendent. Coats of arms and aristocratic insignia may have seen justice done to them by the law of equality; but historians will always take them into account as significant testaments in the search to shed light on the warrior destiny, or ambition, of those ancient Bonapartes.

In fact, was there ever a shield as proud and symbolic as that of these Majorcan knights? That lion rearing up to fight, that sky strewn with stars, from which the eagle is prophetically trying to free himself, is it not like an enigmatic hieroglyphic, hinting at an extraordinary destiny. Napoleon, who was quite superstitious in his love of the poetry of the stars, gave the eagle to France for its emblem. Was he aware of this Majorcan shield then, and not having been able to research his origins as far back as the Bonpars of Provence, kept silent about his Spanish ancestors? It is the fate of all great men to have nations dispute their cradle, or their tomb, after their deaths.

EVIDENCE OF THE NOBILITY OF PERE FORTUNY
(13th June 1549)

FORTUNY
HIS FATHER, OF MAJORCAN LINEAGE

Silver field, five black roundels, two pairs and a solitary.

COS
HIS MOTHER, OF MAJORCAN LINEAGE

Red field, golden bear wearing a fleur-de-lys on its head.

BONAPART
HIS PATERNAL GRANDFATHER, OF MAJORCAN LINEAGE

The description was missing here: the differences arise from the fact that the person who drew this forgot to take into account that it was traced; it is also inaccurate.

GARÍ
HIS MATERNAL GRANDMOTHER, OF MAJORCAN LINEAGE

Field split into red and blue, three silver towers on the red, a pair and a solitary, and on the blue, three wavy lines in silver.

BONAPART

Obtained from an armorial manuscript that contained the coats of arms of the principal families of Majorca, etc. The manuscript belonged to Don Juan Dameto, the chronicler of Majorca, who died in 1633, and is conserved in the library of the Count of Montenegro. The manuscript is from the 16th Century.

Majorca, 20th September 1837.
M. TASTU

154

THIRD PART

CHAPTER ONE

e left for Valldemosa on a calm morning in mid-December, and we took possession of our Carthusian cell among the beautiful rays of an autumn sun, which were to be conspicuous by their absence for us soon after. After crossing the fertile plains of *Establiments*, we reached those ill defined lands, the likes of which I have seen nowhere else: partly covered with woods, partly dry and rocky, partly moist and fresh, and, everywhere, distorted by the primordial movements of the earth.

In no other area, except perhaps in some Pyrenean valleys, had I seen nature so openly reveal its charm to me, as on those quite vast moorlands of Majorca, which brought to my mind an obvious repost to the Majorcan's boastful claim that they have tamed the entire island with crops.

However, I will not reproach them with it; since there is nothing more beautiful than these uncared for lands, that produce all one could want, and do not lack for anything: twisted trees, leaning to protect their frayed leaves; fearsome thorns, magnificent flowers, a carpeting of moss and narcissi, barbed caper bushes, delicate, and charming, long-leafed lilies; all taking on shapes that God pleased to give them, a ravine, a hill, a stony path tumbling suddenly into a gorge, a verdant path disappearing into a risky stream, bare meadows that open out invitingly, until they are unexpectedly blocked by the sheer sides of a mountain; copses dotted with huge rocks that might have fallen from the skies, narrow passes that have been carved out along the paths of streams that pass through myrtle and honeysuckle bushes; finally, a farm, materializing like an oasis in the middle of that desert, its palm tree thrust skywards, like a look-out post to guide the traveller through all of that solitude.

Switzerland and the Tyrol did not have this facet of free and primitive creation, which enchanted me so much in Majorca. It appears to me that in the wildest Helvetian mountains, Nature, free to face the harshest atmospheric conditions, has evaded Man, only to receive even more pitiless treatment at the hands of the weather, and to suffer, like an ardent soul that has liberated itself, the slavery of its own lacerations. In Majorca, Nature flourishes in the embrace of a passionate sky, and smiles beneath the balmy gusts that slap her as they come in off the sea. Flowers that are flattened by the wind, spring up again more robust than ever, the tree trunk, broken by a storm, sends out many more shoots after it is over; and, despite the fact that there are no real deserts on the island, the absence of passable roads give it an air of abandonment, or rebellion which must make it resemble the beautiful savannahs of Louisiana, where in my fondest childhood dreams, I would follow René on the trail of Atala or Chactas.[1]

I am quite sure that this eulogy will not please the Majorcans, who are convinced that they have very pleasant roads. I do not deny that they are agreeable to the eye, but as to whether they are practical for coaches, I will let you decide for yourself, Gentle Reader.

The coach most used locally is the *tartana*, a sort of hackney carriage, having no springs of any kind, which is pulled by a horse, or a mule; also popular is the *birlotxo*, a type of cabriolet for four passengers, which is as well equipped with suspension as the *tartana*. They both have solid wheels and ironwork, and their interiors are padded with six inches of flock wadding. Such rich upholstery certainly makes you think when you first step into this apparently luxurious carriage. The coachman sits on a board, which is the nearest he has to a seat, his

---

[1] Characters from Chateaubriand's novels *René* and *Atala*; works that prefigured the Romantic Movement. (Tr. Note)

feet positioned on each shaft and the hindquarters of the horse between his legs, this allows him to feel not only the movements of his carriage, but also those of his horse, effectively meaning that he is both driving a coach, and riding a horse, at one and the same time. He does not seem to be disheartened by this arrangement, since he sings all the time, no matter what dreadful bumps or jolts he is suffering, and he will only interrupt his recital to occasionally swear foul curses at his mount, if the poor animal hesitates when faced with the edge of a precipice, or before a mound of stones he expects it to cross.

Because that is what one has to face: gulleys, ferocious streams, ruts, swamps, savage hedges, and gaping ditches try to obstruct your passage in vain, the driver does not stop for such trivial considerations. These are what are called roads in Majorca.

When you first set off on one of these apparent obstacle courses, you may think your driver is taking you that way to win some reckless bet and you may ask him what has gotten into him.

"It's the road," he would reply.

"But this stream here?"

"It's the road."

"And that deep hole?"

"The road"

"And that thick undergrowth?"

"Still the road"

"Great!"

You have then no option but to leave everything to

Fate, bless the upholstery, without which you would surely arrive with broken bones, commend your soul to God, and gaze out at the landscape, waiting for imminent death, or a miracle.

Nevertheless, you sometimes arrive safe and sound, thanks to the sturdiness of the carriage, the solidity of the horse's legs, and, perhaps, the unconcern of the driver, who loosens the reins, crosses his arms, and calmly smokes his cigar, while one wheel scrapes against the mountainside, and the other nearly dangles over a cliff.

One becomes accustomed to dangers very quickly, when one sees that others are not worried in the slightest about them; even so, it does not make the danger any less real. The carriages seldom tip over, but when they do, very few step out from underneath. M. Tastu had experienced an accident of this type on the road through *Establiments* the year before, and had been left for dead. As a consequence of that episode, he suffered terrible headaches which, however, still did not dampen his ardour for returning to Majorca.

Most people have some kind of carriage in Majorca, while the nobility have coaches from the era of Louis XIV, with a widened box, some with eight windows, and with enormous wheels that brave any obstacle. These heavy, ungainly vehicles, badly sprung, yet spacious and solid, are agilely pulled along by four or six strong mules, who manage to gallop, with audacity, along the most terrifying narrow gorges, not without giving you a bruise or two, bumps on your head, and leaving you painfully stiff afterwards.

The sombre Miguel de Vargas, a truly Spanish author, who has never made a joke in his life, talks about the *horrendous roads* of Majorca in these terms: "The abandonment of this essential area of public policy in this Balearic isle is to be wondered at. What they call roads are little more than a series of virtually impassable precipices; and on the journey from Palma to the hills of Galatzó, the unhappy passenger dices with death at every step..."

Around the villages, the roads are a little less dangerous, but they have the serious inconvenience of being narrowly restricted between two walls, or two ditches, that prohibit the passing of two carriages. If two vehicles wish to pass, then the bullocks have to be unhitched from the cart, or the horses have to be uncoupled from the carriage, and one of the vehicles has to back up, often quite a distance. This causes interminable arguments as to who should cede passage, and during this time the traveller, already late, can only repeat to himself the Majorcan refrain "*mucha calma*", for his own particular edification.

Although the Majorcans spend almost nothing on the maintenance of their roads, they do have a lot of them. The only problem is choosing which to take. I only made the journey from the Carthusian Monastery to Palma and back three times, but I have travelled six different routes, and on all six the driver of the *birlotxo* lost his way, and we trundled across mountains and through valleys in a supposed search of a seventh route, which we were told was the best of them all, and which we never found.

"Périca" - George Sand's majorcan sevant girl
(drawing by Maurice Sand)

A typical majorcan scene
(drawing by Maurice Sand)

Palma is three leagues from Valldemosa, but three Majorcan leagues, which never took us less than three hours, even when the going was good. The first two ascend, almost imperceptibly; while the third enters the mountains, and climbs up a very even, but very narrow ramp (probably the work of the former Carthusian monks), at a horribly rapid pace, making this section more dangerous than the entire rest of the journey.

Here one starts to appreciate the more Alpine side of Majorca; but in vain, do the mountains rise steeply on each side of the gorge, in vain, do the torrents leap from rock to rock, for it is only in the middle of winter that the landscape acquires anything of the wild aspect the Majorcans attribute to it. In the month of December, and despite recent rains, the torrent was little more than a charming brook, which wended its way through thickets of herbs and flowers; the mountain was cheerful, and the cramped valley of Valldemosa opened out to us, like a spring garden.

In order to get to the monastery, it is necessary to walk up the final hill, since no carriage can manoeuvre along the paved path leading up to the entrance. It is however, a lovely walk, as the path winds sinuously among beautiful trees, and delightful scenery greets you at each step; becoming ever lovelier the higher one goes. I have never seen anything so delightful, and yet so melancholy at the same time, as those landscapes in which the holm oak, the carob, the pine, the olive, the poplar and the cypress blend their varied hues in shady groves, veritable chasms of greenery, where the torrent tumbles its way through thickets of a sumptuous richness and inimitable loveliness. I shall never forget a certain detour the gorge takes where, as I turned around, one of those charming Moorish styled cottages I have described, could be made out up on the higher slopes, half hidden among the broad leaves of the prickly pear and dominated by a great palm tree, that overhangs the abyss, outlining its silhouette against the sky. When the mud and fog of Paris afflict my sight and my spirit, I close my eyes and recall, as if in a dream, that verdant mountain, those fawn coloured rocks, and that solitary palm tree, lost against a rose tinted sky.

The Valldemosa range rises in a series of plateau, narrowing into a kind of funnel, surrounded by high peaks, and closed to the north by the sloping sides of a final plateau, at the entrance to which lies the monastery. Through enormous labour, the monks managed to polish down the roughness of this romantic location. The valley at the end of the range was converted into a vast garden encircled by walls, that barely obstruct the view, and by a line of pyramid shaped cypresses, marshalled in pairs on different planes, which give the place the *contrived* look of a graveyard in an opera.

This garden, planted with palms and almond trees, takes up the entire sloping backdrop of this little valley, and rises up across the lower slopes of the mountain, forming huge terraces, which, by moonlight, when the irregularities of these terraces are camouflaged by shadows; resemble an arena cleaved out of the hillside for combats between giants. In the centre, and beneath a group of beautiful palm trees, there is a stone tank, which collects the waters from the mountain springs, and discharges them into the lower terraces via tiled canals, similar to those that irrigate the outskirts of Barcelona. These works are too considerable and ingenious, both in Majorca and Catalonia, to not be the work of the Moors. They can be found all over the island, but those which leave the monastery garden, following the bed of the torrent, carry fresh water to Palma throughout the year.

Situated on the last pass of the range, the Charterhouse looks out to the north over a spacious valley, which rises up in gentle slopes, and opens out towards the sheer cliffs, which plunge into the waves that batter the coast. The range is orientated towards Spain in one direction, and towards the Orient in the other; thus, this picturesque monastery overlooks the sea on two sides. Whilst the roar of the sea can actually be heard from the northern side of the pass, to the south, far across the immense plane, it can be discerned as a faint glistening line. It is a sublime picture. The foreground is framed by black rocks covered in firs, while the middle-distance is marked by the profiles of mountains, whose outlines are thrown into relief by the magnificent trees along their edge. Towards the background are rounded hillocks, that the setting sun gilds with the warmest hues, and on whose tops can be glimpsed, although they are a league away, the microscopic silhouettes of trees as slender as a butterfly's antennae, and as clear and black as a calligraphic brush stroke in Indian ink, on a field of glittering gold. This luminous backdrop is the plain; and at this distance, when the mountain begins to breathe a mist into the air that covers the chasm in a transparent veil, you could believe it was the sea. However, the sea is in fact further off still, and when the sun rises, the next day, and the plane appears to be a blue lake, the Mediterranean traces a bright silver ribbon to mark off this glorious panorama.

It is one of those views that overwhelm one, because they leave nothing to wish for, nothing to imagine. Everything that the poet or painter could dream of, has been created by nature here in this place. An immense assembly, infinite details, inexhaustible variety, hazy forms, sharp outlines, vague depths, it is all there, and art can add nothing to it. Our understanding is not always adequate to appreciate and understand the works of God, and profound self-contemplation can only lead to a feeling of impotence at being unable to create anything on the immense scale of the fascinating and intoxicating natural world. I would advise anyone who is devoured by the conceit of art to take a long look at such a scene and to do this frequently. I believe that this divine art, which is ever present in creation, would teach them a certain respect for things, which their obsession with form has led me to conclude that they lack.

As for me, I had never felt the vacuity of words as

acutely as in the hours I spent in contemplation at the monastery. I was overpowered by religious impulses; but I was not able to express my enthusiasm in any better form than this: My God, blessed art thou for having given me excellent sight!

However, I believe that while the fortuitous enjoyment of these sublime views is healthy and refreshing, being in continuous possession of them is dangerous. One becomes accustomed to living under the empire of the senses, and the law that governs all excess of feeling is boredom. This explains the indifference of the monks, in general, to the poetry of their monasteries, or the apathy of the peasants and shepherds towards the beauty of their mountains.

We did not have enough time to become tired of it all, because a fog descended to accompany us almost every sunset, shortening still further the brief winter days we enjoyed in that enclosed valley. We were in the shadow of the great mountain to our left until midday, and after three o'clock we became enveloped in the shadow of that to our right. But what beautiful effects of light we were able to observe, when the oblique rays of the sun penetrated the fissures in the rocks, or slid between the mountain ridges, tracing purple and gold crests across the middle-distance! Sometimes our cypresses, black obelisks that provided the foreground of our picture, dipped their tops into this fluidity of light; the date laden stems, dangling from our palm trees, seemed bunches of rubies, and a great shadow line cut the valley diagonally

169

into two areas, one bathing in the clarity of summer, and the other caught beneath the azure chill of a winter landscape.

As the Charterhouse at Valldemosa conformed to Carthusian rules, it once contained exactly thirteen monks, counting the abbot, and so escaped the 1836 decree, which had ordered the demolition of monasteries inhabited by less than twelve members of the community. However, as with all of the others, they still scattered the community, and suppressed the monastery, meaning that it was now considered state property. The Majorcan state, having little idea how to use these vast buildings, had decided that, while waiting for them to fall down, they would hire out the cells to anyone wishing to live in them. Despite the fact that the rents were very moderate indeed, the villagers of Valldemosa had not wished to avail themselves of the opportunity, perhaps due to the extreme piety and nostalgia they had felt towards the monks, or perhaps due to some superstitious fear; which, however, did not prevent them from using the place as a dance hall during carnival, as I will explain later, although it did seem to influence the prejudicial way in which our irreverent presence within those venerable walls was viewed.

Nevertheless, at the height of the hot summer, the monastery is largely inhabited by the petit-bourgeois from Palma, who come to these heights, beneath these thick vaults, in search of the cooler breezes they lack on the plain or in the city. However, as soon as winter approaches they flee the cold, and while we were there, the only inhabitants of the monastery, apart from my family and I, were an apothecary, a sacristan, and Maria Antonia.

Maria Antonia was a kind of caretaker who, I believe, had come from Spain to escape from poverty, and had hired a cell in order to exploit the temporary guests there. Her cell was next to ours, and served as our kitchen, while the lady herself was ostensibly our housekeeper. She had once been beautiful, and was still fine and proper in appearance; she maintained that she was of a good family, and her manners were charming. Her voice was melodious, though perhaps a little insincere, and she practiced a singular style of hospitality. She had the habit of offering her services to all newcomers, but with a hurt expression, nearly burying her head in her hands, refusing all offer of reimbursement for her pains. Her labours were done for the love of God; she would say, and with the sole aim of winning the friendship of her neighbours. For furniture, she had a folding bed, a small heater, a brazier, two chairs with straw seats, a crucifix, and some terracotta plates. She generously placed all of this at your disposition, adding that you could use her cooking pot, or billet your maid under her roof.

However, she viewed the arrangement as reciprocal, and was wont to make use of the best of your clothes and food. I have never before seen as pious a mouth as devoted to eating with such gusto, nor fingers as agile at sampling food from the depths of a boiling pot without scalding herself, nor a throat as voluminous when slyly swallowing the coffee and sugar of her dear guests, while humming a canticle or a bolero. A neutral observer might have found it most amusing to witness the good Antonia, and Catherine, that great Valldemosan witch who served us as a chambermaid and the *niña*, that little dishevelled monster who played at being a maid, squabbling over our dinner. This happened at the hour of the Angelus, which these three cats never stopped mewling, the older women in a duet, picking at every dish as they sang, while the younger chipping in with occasional *amens* while skilfully palming the odd chop or piece of preserved fruit. It was a picture waiting to be painted, and worth the effort of pretending not to have noticed anything. However, when the rains began to interrupt the supply of food from Palma, it began to be harder to see the funny side of the questionable assistance of Maria Antonia and company, and my children and I began to take turns at watching over our groceries. I remember having to hide a basket of biscuits, almost beneath my pillow, that we desperately needed for the following morning's breakfast, or else having to drift in circles around the kitchen, like a vulture, to ward off those lesser birds of prey from raiding the fish on our outdoor stove, and leaving us nothing but bones.

The sacristan was a heavily built young man who had, perhaps, once been an acolyte of the order in his childhood, and who had been the janitor of the place ever since. He had a scandalous past, having confessed to, and been convicted for, seducing and leaving with child a young lady, who had come to stay for a few months in the monastery with her parents. He offered for excuse the fact that the state had only entrusted him to keep the virgins in the paintings unsullied. He was far from handsome, but he liked to put on the airs of a dandy. Instead of the attractive semi-Arab costume that people of his class usually wore, he wore European trousers and braces that really had the local girls swooning. His sister was the most beautiful young Majorcan girl I have ever seen. They did not live in the monastery, they were rich and proud, and had a house in the village; but they did their rounds every day, and came to visit Maria Antonia, who invited them in to taste our food, when she was not hungry herself.

The apothecary was an ex-monk, who sealed himself up alone in his cell in order to put on his white habit, and recite his old offices with great solemnity. Whenever anyone knocked on his door to ask for marshmallow or couch grass (the only medicine he possessed), he would hurriedly stuff his robes under his bed, and appear in short black breeches, tights and a waistcoat, the exact same clothes in which Moliere would once have outfitted the dancers of the ballets in the intervals of his plays. He was a mistrustful old man, who never complained about anything, and perhaps prayed for the triumph of Don Carlos, and the return of the Holy Inquisition, without wishing harm on anyone. He sold us his herbs for their

173

weight in gold, and consoled himself with this modest revenue for having been delivered of his vow of poverty. His cell was located far from ours, near the entrance to the monastery, in a kind of alcove, whose door was hidden behind castor-oil bushes and other abundant medicinal herbs. Hidden there like an old hare terrified of putting the hounds on his scent, he was rarely seen, and had we not gone there on several occasions to ask him for one of his potions, we might never have imagined that there was still a monk left in the charterhouse.

The monastery is no architectural gem, but it is a group of very well built buildings. Its colossal stone walls enclose an area that could house an army corps, and yet it was once home to a mere twelve monks. In the new cloister alone, (the monastery is comprised of three charterhouses from different periods, built one on top of another) there are twelve cells, along one side of the cloister, each containing three spacious rooms. On two of the other sides, there are twelve chapels. Each monk had his own, in which he would retire to pray alone. Each is decorated differently, but they all share a lot of gilt, and a number of paintings realised in the coarsest taste, there are also statues of saints in painted wood that are so horrendous that I confess that I would not have liked to find any of them outside their niches on a dark night. The floors of these private prayer rooms are covered in glazed tiles, making up mosaics with different designs, all to a beautiful effect. Moorish taste is still evident in these floors, and is the only example of good taste that has defied the centuries in Majorca. Finally, each of the chapels has a font, or a basin, in good local marble, as each monk was expected to clean his oratory every day. In these dark vaulted rooms, tiled with mosaics, there is a freshness that must have made the long hours of prayer a positive delight during the scorching hot, dog days.

The fourth side of the new cloister, in whose centre is a small courtyard planted, symmetrically, with boxwood that have still not lost the pyramidal shape the monk's shears cut them into, is parallel to a lovely church whose freshness and cleanliness contrast with the abandonment and solitude of the monastery. We hoped to find an organ there; but we had forgotten that the Carthusians prohibited any kind of musical instrument, as a vain luxury and a pleasure for the senses. The church comprises a single nave, paved in glazed tiles, with artistically arranged bunches of flowers finely painted on them, giving the floor a carpet like effect. The wooden panelling, the confession boxes, and the doors, are of a simple design; but the perfection of the ribs and the neatness of the sober, yet delicate, work that went into the ornamentation, are testament to a skill no longer to be found, even among cabinet makers in France. Unfortunately, this expertise has been lost in Majorca too. M. Tastu assures me that there are only two craftsmen still practicing carpentry as art on the entire island. The chippy that we employed at the monastery was certainly an artist, but only as far as music and painting were concerned. He had come to our cell one

175

day to install some deal shelves, and he scrutinized our limited collection of artistic equipment with a naïve and unsubtle curiosity that I had seen once before on the faces of Greek Slavs. My son had made some sketches, based on some Goya drawings, showing some drunken monks on the town, and decorated the walls of our cell with them, these shocked him somewhat; but when he saw an engraved copy of Rubens' *The Descent from the Cross*, he stood before it for a long time, in a sort of strange contemplation. I asked him what he thought, and he replied in the local dialect: "There is nothing on the whole Island of Majorca that is as beautiful and as natural!"

This word *natural*, in the mouth of a peasant with the manners and mane of a savage, astonished us greatly. The sound of the piano, and the skill of the player, sent him into raptures. He would stop his work, and stand behind the piano stool, with his mouth half open and his eyes bulging. These moments of exaltation did not, however, stop him from being a thief in his dealings with foreigners, a trait that he shared with all Majorcan peasants, who brazenly cheat the stranger without remorse, though I am told they are scrupulously honest among themselves. He charged us a small fortune, and could not keep his greedy hands off all the small French made articles that we had brought with us for personal use. It was with great difficulty that I managed to save some of my toiletry items from his voluminous pockets. What tempted him the most was a cut-glass goblet; either that or the toothbrush that I kept in it, although I very much doubt that he knew the purpose of that particular object. The man had the artistic leanings of an Italian, and the rapacious instincts of a Malay, or a Kaffir.

This digression has not made me forget to mention the sole object of artistic value that we found in the monastery. It was a statue of St Bruno in painted wood, stood in the church. The carving and the painting were remarkable, and the hands were admirably studied, shown in pious and poignant supplication; while the expression on the face, full of suffering and faith, was truly sublime. Yet this was the work of some ignorant artisan, because the statue facing was also carved by the same hand and it was particularly dreadful. The sculptor must have had a moment of sheer inspiration when he carved St Bruno, or perhaps a flash of religious exaltation had caused him to excel himself. I doubt if the fanatical Saint from Grenoble had ever been understood and portrayed with such profound and ardent feeling. Here was the personification of Christian asceticism. But even on Majorca, this symbol of a departed philosophy stands alone.

The ancient cloister, through which one must pass to reach the new one, is attained by taking a simple short cut that my lack of orientation usually led me to miss, causing me to find myself in the third cloister first.

This third building, which we should really call the first cloister, since it is the most ancient, is also the smallest. It is of a charming aspect. The courtyard, encircled by tumbled down walls, was the monks' cemetery. The monks prepared their own tomb during their lives; however, no inscription distinguishes one from another. This was so that nothing could claim to oppose the obliteration of the memory of the occupant by death's oblivion. The graves are only distinguished at all, by the presence of slight bulges among the overgrown grass. M. Laurens has illustrated the physiognomy of this cloister in a beautiful drawing in which I recognised, to my great delight, the little well with its pointed gable, the stone crosses on the windows, festooned with examples of all of the weeds which grow in the ruins, and the great erect cypresses that, at night, resembled black phantoms, standing guard around the white timber cross. It is a pity that he did not see the moon rising behind the beautiful amber coloured sandstone mountain that looms over the cloister, and that he did not choose to put in the foreground that old laurel, with the enormous trunk and the wilted top; perhaps it was no longer there when he visited the Charterhouse. However, I was pleased to see in his drawing, and the accompanying text, an honourable mention for the beautiful miniature palm (*chamoerops*) that I defended against the naturalist passions of my children, and that is, perhaps, one of the most vigorous examples of its kind in Europe.

Around this small cloister are the old chapels of the fifteenth century monastery. They are hermetically sealed, and the sacristan refuses to open them for anyone, which of course aroused our curiosity greatly.

The Charterhouse Valldemossa
(drawing by Maurice Sand)

Palma Cathedral
(drawing by Maurice Sand)

By peering through the cracks while on our walks, we fancied we could discern the vestiges of beautiful pieces of furniture and ancient wooden sculptures. Perhaps these mysterious store rooms contain much buried treasure, which nobody on Majorca will ever bother to brush the dust from.

The second cloister has twelve cells and twelve chapels, like the others. Its crumbling arches still have a lot of character. However, they do not hold anything up now, and whenever we walked among them of an evening, in windy weather, we would commend our souls to God; because there was hardly a storm that did not send some piece of monastery wall or vault crashing down. I have never heard winds so cheerless, howling so desperately, as in those empty, echoing galleries. My memory becomes crowded with the noise from the torrents, the clouds racing by, the monotonous roar of the sea, interrupted by the harsh whistle of the gale, and the laments of sea-birds passing overhead, terrified and disorientated by the great gusts of wind; then the thick fogs, that suddenly fell like a shroud, and which, percolating the cloisters through the broken arches, made us invisible, and made the lamp we carried seem like a mischievous pixy, misguiding us through the galleries, all this, and a thousand other details of that coenobitical existence made that Charterhouse the most romantic dwelling place on earth.

I was not unhappy to see, in reality, and in detail, what I had previously only seen in dreams, or fashionable ballads, or in the nuns' scene from *Robert the Devil* at the opera. Yes, we even had our spectral apparitions, which I will soon describe; and I can add that all of this romanticism parading before our eyes led me to make certain deliberations on the nature of romanticism in general.

To the mass of buildings already described, we should add the part reserved for the abbot, which, like many other mysterious nooks, we were unable to visit; also the cells for the lay brothers, a small church belonging to the ancient Charterhouse, and several other buildings designed for important persons who came there to undertake retreats, or to fulfil penitential devotions; several small courtyards with stables for the community's animals, accommodation for the numerous entourage of visitors, in short, the whole phalanstery, as we would say today, under the protection of the Virgin and Saint Bruno.

When bad weather impeded us from climbing the mountain, we took our constitutionals under cover, within the confines of the monastery. The exploration of this immense mansion would entertain us for hours. I know not what inquisitive impulse kept driving me to discover, within those abandoned walls, the inner secret of monastic life. Its traces were still so fresh, that I often imagined I could hear the shuffle of sandals on the paving, or the murmur of prayers beneath the vaults of the chapels. In our cells, one could still read printed Latin prayers, glued to the walls, even in the most secret crannies, where I would never have imagined anyone had hidden themselves to say the *oremus*.

One day, while exploring the upper stories, we found a beautiful gallery, from which one could look down into a large beautiful chapel. It was so well furnished and tidy, that it looked as if its occupants had left it the day before. The abbot's chair was still in its place, and the order of the week's religious exercises could still be seen within a black wooden frame, hung from an arch in the middle of the chapter stalls. Each stall had a small image of a saint stuck to the back of it, probably the patrons of each former occupant. The smell of incense that had impregnated the walls over centuries had still not completely dissipated. The altars were adorned with dry flowers, and half consumed candles still stood in their candelabras. The orderliness and the state of conservation of these objects contrasted greatly with the ruins outside, the height of the bushes that invaded the windows, and the cries of children who played in the cloisters, using fragments of mosaic for marbles.

As for my children, a sense of wonder drove them into ever more fervent explorations. Of course, my daughter expected to stumble upon some marvellous fairy palace, hidden among the monastery lofts, and my son was on the trail of a clue to some strange and terrifying tragedy, hidden beneath the rubble. I was often alarmed to see them scampering like cats across warped planks, and across shaky balconies; and when they got ahead of me by a few steps, and would disappear around a bend in a spiral staircase, I would imagine I had lost them, and quicken my step with a terror that verged on the superstitious.

It is useless to deny it: those sinister halls, consecrated to a cult even more sinister, do stir up a certain dread in the imagination, and I would defy the calmest and coolest of persons to remain so there for long. Yet little far-fetched fears, if I may call them that, have their attractions; they are certainly real enough to require you to struggle with them within yourself. I confess that I rarely crossed the cloister after dark without a certain emotion, a mixture of uneasiness and delight, although I tried my best not to allow my children to see me in that state, for fear of tainting them with it. They did not appear to be similarly affected and would often enjoy running around those broken arches in the moonlight, which for me seemed the perfect setting for a witches' sabbath. Several times I led them through the cemetery at midnight.

However, I never let them out on their own after we had crossed paths with a tall old man, who occasionally wandered around among the shadowy cloisters. He was an old servant, or dependant, of the monastery who frequently let wine, or religious fervour, go to his head. When he was inebriated, he would stagger around the cloisters, knocking on the doors of empty cells with a great pilgrim's staff, from which hung a long rosary, calling for the monks in drunken bellows, or else mumbling prayers in a lugubrious voice before the chapels. Whenever he saw a light emanating from our cells, he would lurk outside our door, issuing threats, and uttering fearsome oaths. He used to call on Maria Antonia, who was very afraid of him, and deliver long sermons to her, interspersed with foul curses; then he would sit around her brazier until the sacristan arrived to wheedle and cajole him politely out; because the sacristan was not a courageous gentleman and was afraid of making an enemy of him. The fellow would then knock at our door at some ungodly hour, and when he was tired of calling in vain on Father Nicholas, who was his particular obsession, he would slump at the feet of the Madonna, stood in the niche a few paces from our door, and drop off to sleep there, with an open knife in one hand, and a rosary in the other.

His unruly behaviour did not worry us overly, because he was not a man who suddenly leapt on one without warning. He would announce his presence from afar, with his incoherent yelling, and the sound of his staff on the flagstones, giving us enough time to beat a hasty retreat from that savage animal, and the double door of solid oak on our cell could have resisted a far greater siege; but we had an invalid laid low, and in need of rest, and it became very difficult to see the comical side of his persistent assaults. However, we had to suffer these intrusions with *mucha calma*, because, of course, in such a place we would have received no protection from the local police; we did not attend mass, and our enemy was a saint who never skipped a single one.

One night we were disturbed by an apparition of a

very different nature, which I shall never forget. First, there was an unexplainable noise that I can only compare to thousands of sacks of walnuts rolling incessantly over wooden floorboards. We hastened out into the cloister to see what could possibly be causing it. The cloister was dark and deserted, as always, but the noise approached unceasingly, and soon a faint clarity began to whiten the vast profundity of the vaults. Gradually, this became the light from several torches, and then, in the midst of the red smoke they were discharging, appeared a battalion of beings abominable to the sight of God or man. It was no lesser person than Lucifer himself, accompanied by his entire retinue. A lordly devil, all in black, horned with a blood red face, surrounded by a swarm of lesser devils with birds' heads, horse's tails, and gaudy coloured costumes; there were also she-devils or shepherdesses dressed in white and pink dresses, who appeared to have been kidnapped by those evil fiends. After the confessions I recently made above, I have to recognise that for a minute or two, and even for a certain time after I had understood what was going on, I needed an effort of will to hold the lamp up at a steady height to view this ugly masquerade, which the hour, the place, and the torchlight had given a truly Satanic appearance.

It was only some villagers, prosperous farmers, and petit bourgeoisie who were celebrating *Mardi Gras*[2] , and

[2] Shrove Tuesday. As the English speaking world does not particularly celebrate this day, I have left this in the original French, since the Mardi Gras of New Orleans is certainly well-known. It literally means "Fatty Tuesday" and marks the last day of feasting before lent. (Tr. Note).

had come there to perform their folk dances in Maria Antonia's cell. The strange noise that accompanied their parade was the rattle of the castanets, which various young scamps, covered in filthy and ghastly masks, were playing as one, like drum rolls on military snares, rather than the staccato rhythm created with this instrument in Spain. This noise, which also accompanies their dances, is so dry and harsh that one needs to be brave to bear fifteen minutes of it. During their festive processions, they frequently interrupt this noise to sing, in unison, a *corranda*, a simple folk song with a musical phrase that repeats interminably; then the castanets take up their rattle again for another three or four minutes. There is nothing more savage than this way of celebrating by shattering the ear drums knocking two pieces of wood together. The musical phrase, which would amount to nothing by itself, takes on great character, when let out over long intervals by those voices, with their very particular character. When they are at their strongest, they seem the most muted, and when they are most animated, they seem the most languid.

I imagine that the Moors must have sang thus, and M. Tastu, who has researched this very subject, is convinced that the principle Majorcan rhythms, their favourite embellishments, and their general style, in fact, are Moorish in origin.

When we were sailing from Barcelona to Palma, on a mild, dark night, illuminated only by the extraordinary phosphorescence of the ship's wake, everyone on board was sleeping, apart from ourselves and the helmsman, who, to avoid falling asleep like the others, sang the night away, but with a voice so soft and controlled, that you would believe he was either afraid to wake his fellow crewmen, or else half asleep himself. We never tired of listening to his strange airs. They followed rhythms and modulations that did not resemble our traditions in the slightest. He appeared to let his voice randomly wander, like the billows from the ship's smokestack, tossed about, and carried away, on the breeze. It was more a reverie than a song, a kind of unworried digression of the voice, in which thought appeared to play little part, but it followed the rocking of the ship, the gentle lapping of the waves under the paddles, and although it appeared a formless improvisation, it had its sweet and monotonous patterns.

That voice, a true expression of contemplation, had great charm.

When all of the devils approached our cells, they surrounded us and greeted us with courtesy and affability; generally speaking, Majorcan manners are never violent or aggressive. King Beelzebub deigned to address me in Spanish, and told me he was a lawyer. Then to give me a more elevated idea of his personage, he tried to speak to me in French, and wanting to ask me if I was enjoying my stay in the Charterhouse, he translated the Spanish word *cartuxa* for the French word *cartouche*, which produced a slight misunderstanding[3]. But a Majorcan devil is not obliged to speak in every tongue.

Their dances are no livelier than their songs. We followed them into Maria Antonia's cell, decorated with paper lanterns suspended from ivy, which had been hung in loops from one end of the room to the other. The orchestra, consisting of a large and a small guitar, a kind of harsh fiddle, and three or four pairs of castanets, began to play local *jotes* and *fandangos*, which resembled those of Spain, but had more original rhythms, and more audacious turns.

The festival was in honour of Rafael Torres, a rich local landowner, who had married a moderately pretty girl a few days previously. The new bridegroom was the only man condemned to dance, almost the entire evening, face to face, with each of the women, who had to await their turn to be asked. While the pair danced, the entire group, serious and silent, would squat on the floor like Orientals and Africans, even the Mayor with his monk's cowl, and his great black staff with a silver head.

The Majorcan *boleros* have a hereditary solemnity so different from the irreverent charm that one can admire in Andalusia. Men and women extend their arms out, and keep them still, moving their fingers over the

---

[3] The name for a Carthusian Monastery in Catalan is "Cartoixa". The author identifies the word spoken to her as a Spanish word; however, the word she quotes is not Spanish and is probably her attempt to spell the Catalan word. The French expression her companion actually used means *cartridge* in English. Given her own error here, I feel the author was being a little harsh on her diabolic cohort. (Tr. Note)

castanets in a rapid and continuous rhythm. The handsome Raphael danced to clear his conscience. When he had finished his task, he sat, like a dog, among the others, leaving the dance floor to his more devilish companions. A young man, as thin as a wasp, was greeted with the warmest enthusiasm for the firmness of his movements, and for some galvanic leaps he achieved on the spot, carried out without the slightest trace of joy illuminating his face. A huge labourer, cocky and full of himself, tried to kick out his leg with his hands on his hips, in the Spanish style, but was very rightly jeered, as he was the most ridiculous figure one could imagine. We would have been entertained by these country dances for longer, if it was not for the reek of rancid oil and garlic that those men and women exuded, a stench that literally stuck in one's throat.

The Carnival outfits occupied far less of our interest than the local Majorcan traditional costume; these were very elegant and refined. The women wore a kind of muslin, or lace, shawl known as a *rebosillo*, composed of two pieces; one is fitted a little towards the back of the head and passes underneath the chin like a nun's coif, this is known as the *rebosillo en amunt*, while the other the *rebosillo en volant* floats loosely over the shoulders rather like a cape. Their hair is parted in the middle, and sleeked down onto the back of the head where it is entwined into a thick plait that protrudes from the *rebosillo*, this then hangs down the back, and is turned up upon itself to one side, and held in place by a belt. On working days, the hair is not plaited, but left loose to dangle down the back in *estufada* style. The bodice, in merino wool, or in black silk, has a low neckline and short sleeves; it is ornamented below the elbow and on the seams along the back with metal buttons, through which silver chains are tastefully and elegantly threaded. The ladies have slim waists, and are well proportioned; their feet are small and carefully shod on festival days. A simple village girl will wear lacy stockings, satin shoes, a gold chain around her neck, and fathoms of silver chain which the girls hang from their bodices and belts. I saw many well-proportioned Majorcan girls, but few who were pretty; their features were regular, like the maids of Andalusia, but their expressions were generally more candid and affable. The women of the Soller district, which I did not visit, have the reputation of being great beauties.

The men that I saw were not handsome, although, at first sight, they all appeared so, thanks to the fetching clothes they wore. Their Sunday best consisted of a heart-shaped *guardapits*, or waistcoat, in multi-coloured silk, worn open at the chest, as is the *saio*, a short, black jacket, drawn in at the waist like a woman's bodice. A dazzling white shirt, gathered at the neck and the sleeves by embroidered tapes, leaves the throat bare and the chest resplendent in fine linen, which always shows clothes off to their best advantage. They tie a coloured sash around their waists, wear locally-made, Turkish-style, baggy britches in striped cotton, or silk. Below this, they wear black, white, or fawn coloured stockings, and shoes in a calf-skin that has neither been sized nor dyed. They sport a wide-brimmed hat, made from *moixi* or wild cat fur. It has black ribbons and tassels, threaded in gold and silk, which rather detracts from the Oriental effect of the rest of their outfit. At home, they wrap a scarf, or a large kerchief, around their heads like a turban, which suits them far more. In winter, they often wear a black woollen skull cap, that covers their tonsure, because, like monks, they shave the tops of their heads; perhaps as a gesture towards cleanliness (although God knows that does not get them very far), or perhaps for religious reasons. Their thick, rough, curly manes drift (if a mane can be said to drift) over the back of their necks. This haircut, exactly like those popular in the Middle Ages, is completed by a straight fringe across the forehead; it is a style which gives dynamism to all who wear it.

In the fields they wear more informal clothes, which are even more picturesque. They bare their legs, or else cover them up to the knees with sallow-coloured leather gaiters, depending on the season. When it is hot, they only wear a shirt and baggy breeches. In winter, they cover themselves with a grey cape that resembles a monk's habit somewhat, or in a large African goatskin, with the fur on the outside. When they walk around in groups, wearing these fawn coloured skins with a black stripe down the back, it is easy to mistake them for a herd of goats, walking along on their hind legs. When they are going off to the fields, or returning home from them, they nearly always have someone walking along at the head of the column, playing a guitar or a flute, the others following in silence, looking at the ground with an innocent, or stupid, expression on their faces. However, they are not without cunning, and anyone who is misled by their appearance would be a fool.

They are generally tall, and the clothes they wear make them appear thin, which in turn makes them appear even taller. They always leave their necks, which are attractive and strong, open to the elements, their chests, free of close-fitting waistcoats and braces, open and well-developed; however, nearly all of them have bandy legs.

We have observed that the elderly and more mature men, without being handsome, all appear to possess gravity and nobility. They all resemble monks, as they are poetically conceived; whereas to us, the younger generation seemed vulgar and more licentious, as if they represented a sudden break in lineage. Is it not some twenty years since the monks ceased to exercise their influence in the intimacies of the home?

This is just a traveller's jest.

CHAPTER TWO

 mentioned earlier that I was searching for the inner secret of monastic life, in a place where the traces of it were still fresh. I do not mean to imply that I expected to discover mysterious deeds connected with this individual Charterhouse; rather, that I invited those forsaken walls to reveal to me the intimate thoughts of the silent inmates, who for centuries had been kept behind them, isolated from the normal lives of their fellows. I would have liked to follow the frayed, or broken thread of the Christian faith in the souls that each generation had abandoned there, like sacrifices to a jealous God, who, like barbarian deities,

had a hunger for human victims. Then, I would have liked to resurrect a fifteenth century monk, and a nineteenth century one, (both Catholics, but without being aware of it, both with very different interpretations of the faith), and ask each one what he thought of the other.

I think the life of the former would be quite easy to accurately reconstruct in my mind. I picture that medieval Christian as a complete person, fervent, sincere, struck to the heart by the wars, discords, and suffering that were the lot of his contemporaries; fleeing from that evil abyss, and seeking, through ascetic contemplation, to disengage himself, as much as possible, from a life in which the notion of the perfectibility of the masses was not yet graspable by individuals. The nineteenth century monk, I found harder to visualise. I envisage him turning a blind eye to the, now, clearly perceivable march of humanity; indifferent to the lives of others, no longer understanding religion, the Pope, the Church, society at large, or even himself; seeing in the Charterhouse no more than a pleasant, safe and spacious dwelling; his vocation offering him nothing more than an guaranteed livelihood, impunity for his baser instincts, and a means of obtaining, without deserving them, the respect and esteem of the pious, the peasant, and women. I found it hard to imagine what degree of repentance, blindness, hypocrisy, or sincerity he must have felt. It was impossible that such a man could have genuine faith in the Church of Rome, unless he were completely lacking in intelligence. It would also be impossible for him to have been a complete non-believer; since, then, his entire life would have been a loathsome lie, and I find it difficult to believe any man can be completely stupid, or completely despicable. I imagined the private hell of his interior struggles, his alternating moods of rebellion and submission, of philosophical doubt, and superstitious terror, and the more I identified myself with the last monk to inhabit my cell before me, the more my imagination became engrossed in the sufferings, and anxieties, I ascribed to him.

It is enough to cast one's eyes over the ancient cloisters and the modern Charterhouse, to see the progress made in improving the wellbeing, health, and even the sophistication of the monk's lives, but, also, to observe the relaxation of the former harsh rules of monastic life, and the decline of the spirit of mortification, and penitence. While the old cells were totally dark, constricted, and draughty, the new ones were airy, bright, and well-constructed. Notwithstanding, I will describe the cell in which we lived, in order to illustrate the austerity of the Carthusian order, even when its severity had been evaded and assuaged, as much as possible.

It comprised three spacious, elegantly arched rooms, ventilated at one end by rosettes, each one different from its neighbour, and all with beautiful designs. These three rooms were separated from the cloister by a dark, curved passageway, closed off by a swinging door in solid oak.

The walls were three feet thick. The room in the middle was designed as a study, or for prayers and meditation, and the only furniture in it was a large bench, six or eight feet long, which was built into the wall, and had a back rest, and a bar on which to kneel to pray. The room to the right of this was the bedroom; at the end of which was a low alcove, tiled above with flagstones, like a sepulchre. The room on the left was the monk's workshop, refectory, and storeroom. A closet, at the back, had a wooden compartment, with a hatch that opened out onto the cloister like a skylight, and which was where the monk's food would be handed in to him. The kitchen consisted of two small stoves, to be found outside the cell, but not, in strict accordance with the rule, in the open air. An arched entranceway, that allowed access into the garden, protected the person cooking from the rain, and thus allowed him to dedicate rather more time to the job than the founder of the order probably would have wished. A fireplace in the third room demonstrated further the relaxation of the rules; although the architect's skills had not extended to designing a chimney that worked efficiently.

At the back of the accommodation, at the height of the rosettes, there was a long, dark, narrow, aisle designed to aid the ventilation of the cell, and above this there was a loft for storing corn, onions, beans, and other frugal provisions for winter. Towards the south, the rooms opened onto a small garden which was exactly the same size as the combined area of the three rooms of the cell, and which was separated from the neighbouring gardens by ten foot high walls, and supported by a solidly built veranda. This overlooked an orange grove that occupied the same level on the mountain terraces. The lower tier of the terraces were covered in vines, the third level with almond trees and palms, and so on, right down into the valley, which, as I have noted previously, seemed one vast garden.

On the right, along the entire length of each monk's garden, there was a chiselled-stone water trough, three or four feet wide, by as many deep, which received water from the mountain streams through open canals in the balustrade of the terrace. These canals then formed a cross shape, which distributed the water into the gardens, dividing each one into four equal sections. I never understood why so much water was required to quench the thirst of one man, or why such an abundance of irrigation was needed for a patch of land some twenty feet across. If I had not been familiar with the horror that the monks expressed towards bathing, and above all with Majorcan habits in this regard, I would perhaps have been led to believe that the good Carthusians spent their lives in ablutions like their Indian counterparts.

These small gardens were planted with pomegranate, and lemon trees, and orange trees, surrounded by raised brick walkways, shaded, like the water trough, by a fragrant covering of foliage. The effect was that of a pretty salon, full of flowers and greenery, where the monk could stroll, dry shod on wet days, and refresh his lawn with a cascade of running water during scorching hot days. Standing by the side of a delightful terrace, he could imbibe the perfume of the orange trees, whose exuberant crowns formed a spectacular dome of flowers and fruit above him, gazing off in complete tranquillity across the austere, yet charming, melancholic, yet breathtaking landscape, which I have already described. He could also grow rare, and precious flowers for the pleasure of his eyes alone, harvest the tastiest fruits with which to quench his thirst, listen to the sublime echo of the sea, contemplate the splendour of summer nights beneath a magnificent sky, and worship the Eternal within the most beautiful temple that man has ever created with the tools of nature.

Such were the ineffable pleasures that I had imagined, at first, for the monks; and such were those that I promised myself, when I moved into one of those cells. Cells that appeared more than willing to co-operate in satisfying the magnificent caprices of the imagination, and the dreams of a chosen community of poets and artists.

However, when one imagines the life of a man without intelligence, and thus unable to dream or meditate, perhaps without faith, in other words, without enthusiasm or devotion, imprisoned within the mute, silent, solid walls of that cell, subject to the stultifying privations of the monastic rule, and forced to observe it to the letter, without understanding its spirit, condemned to the horror of solitude, reduced to viewing his fellow humans from a distance, from the top of a mountain, whence they appear mere ants crawling around the valley floor; permanently isolated from the other captive souls, vowed to the same silence, enclosed in the same tomb, always neighbours, and never communal, even in prayer; in short when one whose mind and body are free is drawn into empathising with certain of these monks' terrors and sufferings, it can only make the life they led seem dispiriting and dark, an empty life full of error and impotence.

Then one can understand the endless tedium of that monk, for whom the appeal of the most beautiful spectacles of nature has worn off, who cannot enjoy them, because he has no one to share the pleasure with; the brutish melancholy of this penitent, who no longer suffers anything but the cold or the heat, like an animal, like a plant; and the moral decay of the spirit of this Christian, whose spirit of asceticism could not be revived by anything in heaven or on Earth. Condemned to eat alone, work alone, suffer and pray in silence, they must have shared one overriding thought, that of escaping such a dreadful imprisonment. Indeed, I am told that the last generation of monks often disappeared, and that some of them absented themselves for weeks, and even months, without the abbot being able to recall them to the Order.

I fear that I have given a long and detailed description of our Charterhouse, without giving the reader the least idea of what had captivated us about the place at first sight, of the poetry we conceived there; before that too dissipated through familiarity. I have surrendered, as I always do, to the influence of my memories, and now that I have tried to communicate my impressions, I ask myself why I have not been able to say in twenty lines what I have taken twenty pages to express, namely that peace of mind, and all that that implies, appear most appetising to the weary soul, but given time for reflection, the attraction soon evaporates. In fact, only a genius can create a vivid and complete picture, using a single brush stroke. When M. Lamennais visited the Camaldolese monastery in Tivoli, he had the same feeling, and expressed it with masterful elegance:

"We arrived at the hour of communal prayer," he states. "All of the monks appeared to be of an advanced age, and unusually tall. Lined up on both sides of the nave, they remained on their knees after their offices, immobile, in deep meditation. One would have thought that they were no longer of this Earth, their shaven heads turned to other thoughts and preoccupations; there was no sign of movement, no outward sign of life; wrapped in their long white habits, they looked like those statues that can be seen praying over old tombs.

"We understood very well the attraction that this solitary existence could have for some exhausted and disillusioned souls. Who has never aspired to something similar? Who has never turned their thoughts towards a desert, or dreamed of reposing in some quiet wood, or in a cave on the mountainside, close to a hidden spring, in which only the birds of the air come to quench their thirst.

"Nevertheless, this is not the true destiny of man, who was born for action; who has his task that must be performed. What matter if it is difficult? Is it not a task dedicated to love?" (*Affairs of Rome*).

This short extract, so full of images and aspirations, ideas and profound reflections, inserted, as if by chance, in a piece M. Lamennais wrote about his dealings with the Holy See, has always impressed me. I am convinced that, one day, some painter will take it as the subject of a painting. On one side the monks at prayer, sombre, placid, forever useless, forever impotent, weary ghosts, the final manifestations of a cult about to enter into the dark night of the past; men as cold and gloomy as the stones paving the tomb they kneel upon. On the other side, the man of the future, the last priest, driven by the last spark of inspiration left in the Church, meditating on the fate of those monks, looking at them with an artist's eye, judging them as a philosopher would. Here, Death's Levites, immobile beneath their shrouds; there, the apostle of life, untiring traveller through the limitless fields of thought, already giving a last understanding farewell to the poetry of the cloister, and shaking from his feet the dust of the city of the popes, so as to stride off on the holy path to moral freedom.

I have not managed to gather any other historical evidence connected with our Charterhouse, except for a sermon of Saint Vincent Ferrer, delivered in Valldemosa in 1413; the accuracy of which I owe, once again, to M. Tastu. This sermon, which was the event of the year in Majorca, illustrates perfectly the eagerness with which a missionary of that period was desired, and the solemnity with which he was welcomed.

"In the year 1409, the Majorcan Great Assembly resolved to write to the great master Vincent Ferrer, or Ferrier, inviting him to come and preach in Majorca. However, it was Don Louis de Prades, Bishop of Majorca, Cardinal Camerlengo[1] of Pope Benedict XIII (the anti-pope Peter de Luna), who, in 1412, wrote to the panel of judges of Valencia, imploring the aid of Master Vincent, and who, the following year, waited for him in Barcelona and embarked with him for Palma. The morning following his arrival, the holy missionary began preaching, and organising nocturnal processions. There was a terrible drought on the island, but after Master Vincent's third sermon, it began to rain. The following details were sent to King Ferdinand by his royal procurator, Don Pedro de Casaldaguila.

"Your Royal Highness, my Most Victorious Prince and Lord, I have the honour to announce to you that Master Vincent arrived in this city on the first day of September, and was received solemnly. On Saturday, in the morning, he began to preach before an immense multitude, which listened to him with great devotion.

---

1 The Cardinal Camerlengo is a member of the Sacred College of Cardinals. On the death of a pope, his task is to take over the stewardship of the church, pending the election of a new pope. (Tr. Note)

Every night thereafter, there have been processions in which men, women and children flagellated themselves. For a long time, there had been no water falling from the skies, but after the third sermon, Our Lord God, moved by the prayers of the children and the people, wished this land, which had suffered great drought, to see a great abundance of rain falling across the entire island, which has caused great rejoicing among the inhabitants.

"Hoping that Our Lord God grant you many long years of life, Most Victorious Lord and that He glorify your royal crown.

"Majorca, 11th September 1413."

"The crowds wishing to hear the holy missionary speak grew too big for the vast church in the monastery of Saint Dominic, so an immense garden in the monastery had to be made available, and stalls had to be erected, and walls torn down.

"Vincent Ferrer preached in Palma until 3rd of October, after which he left to visit the rest of the island. His first stop was in Valldemosa, in the monastery which was to receive and welcome him, and which he had doubtless chosen in consideration of his brother Boniface, who was a General of the Carthusian Order. The abbot of Valldemosa went to Palma to collect him, and travelled with him. In Valldemosa, even more than in Palma, the church was far too small to contain the avid crowds."

Here is what the chroniclers stated:

"The town of Valldemosa preserves the memory of

when Saint Vincent Ferrer sowed the divine word within her. Within the boundaries of the town is found an estate with the name *Son Gual*; to there retired the missionary, followed by a great multitude. The terrain was vast, and flat, and the hollow trunk of a huge ancient olive tree became his pulpit. While the saint preached from the height of his olive tree, it began to rain in abundance. The Devil, great creator of winds, lightning and thunder, appeared to want the listeners to abandon the place, and seek shelter, which, indeed, some of those present began to do. Saint Vincent ordered that nobody move, and started to pray, whereupon a cloud immediately spread over him and the congregation like a canopy; while those who had stayed in the nearby fields were obliged to abandon their labours.

"The ancient tree trunk was still in existence less than a century ago, since our forefathers had religiously preserved it. Then, later heirs to *Son Gual* neglected their duty towards this sacred object and its memory was lost. However, God did not wish for Saint Vincent's improvised pulpit to be lost forever. One day, some servants, who worked on the estate, came looking for firewood, they noticed the trunk and proposed to chop it up; but their tools broke as soon as they tried to cut it. When news of the event spread to the older inhabitants, they claimed it was a miracle, and the sacred trunk was spared. Later, it appears that the trunk split into thirty four pieces; yet although it was not far from the village, nobody dared to touch them, respecting them as they would a relic.

"The holy man also preached in even tiny villages, healing the body and spirit of the unfortunate. The water from a spring that flows near Valldemosa was the only remedy suggested by the saint. This spring, or pool, is still known today by the name *Sa Bassa Ferrera*.

"Saint Vincent spent six months on the island, from whence he was recalled by King Ferdinand of Aragon, to help him extinguish the schism that raged throughout the Occident. The missionary saint bid farewell to the Majorcans with a sermon he preached on the 22nd February 1414 in the Cathedral of Palma. After blessing the congregation, he departed towards his ship, accompanied by the judiciary, the nobility, and a great crowd of common people, performing many miracles on the way, as the chroniclers recount, and as tradition maintains in the Balearics today."

This account, which would make Miss Fanny Elssler[2] smile, gave rise to the following observation by M. Tastu, that is curious in two ways: firstly, because it provides a possible natural explanation for one of the miracles of Saint Vincent Ferrer; secondly, because it confirms a very important piece of linguistic history. Here is what he says:

"Vincent Ferrer wrote his sermons in Latin, and delivered them in the Limousine tongue. It has been considered miraculous that the saint had the power to make his listeners understand him, even though they were being addressed in a foreign language. However,

---

[2] Fanny Elssler (1810-1884) a dancer who introduced elements of folk dance to the classical ballet of her day, most famous for her role as a gipsy. (Tr. Note)

this becomes less miraculous, if one casts one's mind back to the age in which the saint flourished. At that time, the Romance language spoken in the great regions of the North, Centre and South of Western Europe, was practically identical; the people, and above all the learned, understood each other very well. Master Vincent was a success in England, Scotland, Ireland, Paris, Brittany, Italy, Spain and the Balearics; for the reason that the inhabitants of these countries understood, even if they did not necessarily speak, a Romance language which was closely related to the Valencian language, Vincent Ferrer's mother tongue.

"It must be remembered, too, that the celebrated missionary was the contemporary of the poet Chaucer, of Jean Froissart, Christine de Pisan, Boccacio, Ausias March and many other celebrated Europeans"[3]

---

[3] The people of the Balearics speak the ancient Romance tongue of Limousine, a language which M. Raynouard, without research or discrimination, concludes is Provençal. Due to its isolation on these islands, Majorcan has undergone fewer changes than the other Romance languages, and has been less influenced by foreign tongues. The closest parallel to Majorcan is the Langue d'Oc, today in its decline as the charming dialect of Montpellier and its surrounds. This can be explained by the frequent stays of the Kings of Aragon, and their courts, in Montpellier. Peter II, killed in combat with Simon de Montfort at Muret (1213), was married to Marie, daughter of a Count of Montpellier, and their issue was James I, known as the Conqueror, who was born in the town, and spent the first years of his childhood there. One of the characteristics that distinguishes the Majorcan language from other Romance dialects of the Langue d'Oc, are the articles in popular use, and which, curiously, are found in areas of Sardinia. Apart from the masculine articles *lo*, and the feminine article *la*, Majorcan has the following articles:

Masculine Singular: *so*;	Plural *sos*
Feminine Singular: *sa*;	Plural *ses*
Masc. and Fem. Singular: *es*;	Plural *els*

Masculine Singular: *en*
Feminine Singular: *na*
Feminine Plural: *nes*

It is worth noting that these articles, although long in popular use, have never been employed in official documents dating back to the conquest of the Balearics by the House of Aragon. This would appear to indicate that in these isles, as in the Italic lands, there were two languages being spoken simultaneously: *plebea*, the tongue of the common people (which changes little), and *aulica illustre*, the language of learning and literature, which is improved, and refined, over time, by changes in culture, or by works of genius. This is still the case today, where Spanish is the official language throughout Spain, but where every region has kept its dialect, for everyday use. In Majorca, Spanish is only used in formal situations; in everyday situations people use Majorcan, whether among the rich, or the common peasants. If you pass by the balcony of a young girl, an *Al·lote* (from the Moorish *aila*, *lella*), may be seen watering her flowers, and singing, in her sweet national tongue:

Sas al·lotes, tots els diumenges,	The maidens of a Sunday,
Quan no tenen res mes que fer,	With nothing better to do.
Van a regar es claveller	Go water their carnations
Dient-li: Beu, ja que no menges!	Saying: Drink! Since you do not eat.

The music that accompanies these words, is of a Moorish rhythm and cadence, that stirs you and makes you dream. Nevertheless, the girl's mother, adds cautiously:

Al·lotes, filau, filau!	Maidens, spin, spin!
Que su camisa se ru;	Your blouses are worn (literally: Your blouses laugh)
I si no l'apedaçau,	And if you do not patch them
No v's arribara a s'estiu!	They will not last until summer.

Majorcan, especially when spoken by young girls, has a particular charm for the ear of the foreigner. When a Majorcan maid says the following words to you: "Bona nit tenga! Es meu cor no basta per dir-li adios" (Goodnight, my heart is not enough to bid you farewell). It seems as if the soft cantilena could be taken down as a musical phrase.

After these examples of Majorcan vernacular, allow me to quote an example of the ancient academic tongue. The Majorcan Merchant, a fourteenth century troubadour, sang of the rigours of his lady and bid farewell to her thus:

Cercats d'uy may, ja siats bella e pros,
'quel vostres pres, e laus, e ris plesents,
> *Car vengut es lo temps que m'aurets mens.*
> *No m'aucira vostre 'sguard amoros,*
> *Ne la semblança gaya;*

Car trobat n'ay
> *Altra qui m'play*
> *Sol qui lui playa!*
> *Altra, sens vos, per que l'in volray be,*
> *E tindre'en car s'amor, que 'xi s'conve.*

Seek, elsewhere from now on, though you be beautiful and noble,
Those entreaties, praises and smiles that were once for you,
For the moment has arrived in which you shall have fewer.
Your look of love shall no longer cut me to the core,
Nor your joyful countenance.
> For I have found
> Another who suits me
> If I only can suit her
> Another, without you, who I may love the more
> And appreciate her love, which is as it should be.

Like all other Southern peoples, the Majorcans are natural poets and musicians, or as their ancestors would have it, troubadours, a word which could be translated as improvisers. In the island of Majorca there are still many of these, who enjoy local fame, among which are two who live in Soller. These troubadours are commonly visited by happy, or unhappy, lovers who pay the troubadour to sing beneath the balcony of their beloved, late at night, having first primed them with information about her. They sing improvised *cobles* in eulogy, or complaint, or even occasional abuse, based on what the lover has told them. Foreigners can also make use of this service, since on the island of Majorca it is not regarded as leading to any repercussions. (Note by M. Tastu).

[Majorcan is today defined as a dialect of Catalan. However, from personal experience I can vouch for the main thrust of M. Tastu's argument. I have spoken Catalan to people in Southern France and Northern Italy who replied to me in their local Provençal dialects; despite some differences we had no real problems communicating.
Note: Errors in the original orthography in relation to Majorcan have been amended in accordance with current Catalan practice. Tr. Note]

CHAPTER THREE

cannot continue my narrative, without quoting from the devotional annals of Valldemosa; since in mentioning the fanatical piety of the villagers with whom we associated, I must inevitably mention the saint of whom they are so proud, and whose cottage they showed us.

"Valldemosa is also the hometown of Catalina Tomas, beatified in 1792 by Pope Pious VI. The life of this saintly maiden has been written many times, the latest version being the work of Cardinal Antoni Despuig. Her story is not without its charming naivety. The legend states that, as God had favoured this maiden with exceptional discernment, she was eager to rigorously observe all the fast days, long before she reached the age when the church insisted these should be kept. From her earliest childhood, she abstained from eating more than one meal a day. Her devotion to the passion of Our Redeemer, and the sorrows of His holy Mother was so fervent, that as she walked along she continually recited the rosary, using leaves from lentil plants, or olive trees to count the decades. Her preference for retreats and religious exercises, and the distance she kept from dances and profane amusement, led to her being nicknamed the *velleta* (little old woman). However, her solitude and her abstinence were rewarded by visits from angels, and the Celestial Host: Jesus Christ, His Mother and the saints became her servants; Mary cured her illnesses, Saint Bruno lifted her up whenever she fell; Saint Anthony escorted her through the darkness of the night, carrying her water jug and filling it from the spring; Saint Catherine, her patron, combed her hair, and took care of her like a watchful and concerned mother; Saint Cosmo and Saint Damian cured the wounds she received in her struggles with the Devil, her victory not being achieved without a battle, and, finally, Saint Paul and Saint Peter stood at either side of her, to keep her from temptation.

"She became an Augustinian nun in the convent of Saint Magdalene in Palma, and became an example to the penitents, because, as the Church demands, she was obedient, poor, chaste, and humble. Her biographers attribute the gifts of prophecy and miracle making to her.

They recall how public prayers were being said in Majorca for the health of Pope Pious V, until Catalina suddenly interrupted them, declaring that they were no longer necessary, since the pontiff had just that moment departed this life, which turned out to be true.

"She died on the 5th April 1574, uttering the words of the psalmist: 'Lord, into thy hands I commend my spirit'.

"Her death was considered a public calamity and she was granted the highest honours. Joana de Pochs, a pious lady of Majorca, replaced the wooden coffin, into which the saintly maiden had at first been placed, with a magnificent alabaster sepulchre that she ordered from Genoa; in her will she also left provision for masses to be said on the day of the blessed saint's passing, and on Saint Catherine's day; and desired that a light perpetually burn over her tomb.

"The body of this saintly girl is still preserved today in the Convent of Saint Eulalia, where Cardinal Despuig dedicated an altar and a religious service to her."[1]

I have gladly reported the full text of this little legend, because it is far from my mind to deny the idea of sanctity, and I mean here the true sanctity of the ardent soul. Although the enthusiasm, and the visions, of this little mountain girl of Valldemosa no longer have the same religious sense or philosophical value as the inspirations and ecstasies of the saints from Christianity's golden age, the *velleta* Tomas is still a close

---

[1] Note by M. Tastu (Author's Note)

The author must have been given false information, since the body of the young Saint in fact lies in Saint Magdalene's convent, where she was a nun. (Tr. Note)

cousin to the poetic shepherdess Genevieve, and the sublime shepherdess Joan of Arc. The Church of Rome has always reserved places of honour in the heavenly kingdom for the most humble children of the people; even if it now condemns and rejects those apostles who wish to improve the lot of the people here on Earth. Catalina, the *pagesa*[2], was *obedient*, *chaste*, *poor* and *humble*: the peasants of Valldemosa barely benefit from her example, and understand her life so little, that one day they tried to stone my children, because my son was drawing the grounds of the monastery, which they took as a desecration. Like the Church, with one hand they lit the bonfires of the *auto da fe*, and with the other they burned incense before the effigies of their saints.

The village of Valldemosa is proud of its title of *town*, which dates from the era of the Moors.[3] It is situated on the slopes of the mountain, at the same level as the Charterhouse, of which it appears to be an annex. It resembles a mass of terns' nests, and is almost equally as inaccessible. Its inhabitants are largely fishermen, who go out to sea in the early morning and do not return until nightfall. During the day, the town is full of women, the most gossipy in the world, who can be seen in the doorways of their houses mending their husbands' nets,

[2] *Pages*, *Pagesa* is the name given to anyone from the third class of Majorcan society. The first class are the *cavallers* (nobility), the second class are the *menastrals* (artisans), and the term *pages* (peasant) is used to describe anyone who earns their livelihood from the land. (Author's Note).

[3] The Arabs called it *Villa Avente*, a Roman name that I believe it received from the Pisans or the Genovese. (Author's Note).

or darning their socks, and invariably singing. They are as pious as their husbands; but their piety is less intolerant, because it is more sincere. In this respect, the women of Valldemosa are like women everywhere. In general, women are far more enthusiastic about religious practices or convictions, while with men there is often a question of ambition, or self-interest, at stake. Proof of this has been offered by France during the reigns of Louis XVIII and Charles X, when great and lesser posts in the administration and the army could be bought with a promissory note for a confession, or a mass.

The Majorcans' attachment to the monks is based on greed; and the best witness to this statement is M. Marliani, whose words count for more when we consider that this historian of Modern Spain has expressed his opposition to the measures of 1836, when the monasteries were suddenly dissolved.

"As good landlords," he says. "the monks were not worried about wealth, but had created a real mutual interest between themselves and the peasantry; tenant-farmers cultivating monastery land suffered no great hardships, either in relation to the quotas they had to pay, or the regularity of such payments. The monks, having no heirs, did not accumulate riches, and as soon as they received enough to keep their community operative, they did not see any need to pressurize the peasantry for more. The abrupt dismantling of the monasteries was a threat to the laziness and self-interest of the peasant; they understood only too well that the government and the new landowners would be far more demanding than a community of parasites without family, or social interests. The beggars who swarmed at the refectory doors would also stop receiving the leftovers from those well-fed, idle loafers.

The Carlism of the peasants can only be explained by material needs; because it is impossible to imagine a region less linked to Spain by patriotic sentiment than Majorca, nor a population less inclined to be moved by political exhortations. While taking secret vows to restore the old order, they were terrified of any new disorder, whatever it was. The alarm that had put the island under a state of siege at the time we were there had terrified both the supporters of Don Carlos, and the defenders of Queen Isabel. This alarm was indicative of, I will not say their cowardice (I believe them very capable of making good soldiers), but rather the anxiety produced by their worries over their property, and their selfish desire for a quiet life.

An old priest dreamed one night that his house was being broken into by thieves; he woke terrified. Still affected by the nightmare, he woke his serving woman; she, perceiving his terror without knowing what had caused it, aroused the entire neighbourhood with her screams. The alarm spread like wildfire throughout the village, and then all over the island. Soon, everyone was talking about a Carlist invasion, and the Governor received the declaration of the priest, who, partly from shame of losing face, and partly out of the delirium of a troubled soul, confirmed that he had seen the Carlist advance party. Measures were immediately taken to face the danger; Palma was declared under a state of siege, and all the military forces were put on a state of alert.

However, nobody appeared, nothing moved, not even a bush; like on Crusoe's isle, there was not a foreign footprint visible on the sandy shore. The authorities punished the poor priest for making fools out of them, but instead of sending him packing as a dreamer, they sent him to prison as a seditionist. However, the precautionary measures were not revoked, and when we left Majorca, during the period of the Maroto executions, the state of siege was still in force.

There is nothing as strange as the air of mystery with which the Majorcans enshrouded the events which were then tearing apart the fabric of Spain. Nobody spoke of them, except among their families or in low voices. In a country in which there is no malevolence or tyranny, we found it difficult to accept such shadowy mistrust. I have seldom read anything as funny as the newspaper articles of Palma at the time, and I have often regretted not having cut some out as perfect examples of the Majorcan controversy. However, without exaggeration, the following represents the kind of comment made on the authenticity, and nature, of events by these journals:

"However proven these facts might appear to people predisposed to give them credit, we cannot stress enough our advice to our readers to await the outcome before judging them. Reflections on such events require mature consideration, while awaiting to discover the truth, which we do not wish to convert into doubt, yet nor do we wish to anticipate with imprudent assertions. The destiny of Spain is shrouded in a veil that will not be long in lifting, but which no imprudent hand should attempt to lift before time. We refrain, until then, from publishing our opinion and advise all wise souls not to pronounce on the different acts of the various parties until they have seen the situation more clearly." etc.

Prudence and reserve are the dominant characteristics of the Majorcan disposition, as they are the first to recognise. You never meet a peasant in a field who will not respond to your greeting; however, if you do not know them, and you happen to say one more word to them, they will be very careful what they reply to you, even if you speak to them in their dialect. It is enough that you have the look of a foreigner about you for them to fear you, and to go out of their way to avoid you.

It would have been far easier for us to have lived on better terms with these good people, had we only attended their church services; not that that would have stopped them robbing us blind whenever they could, but we would then have been able to stroll through their fields, without peril of having a stone thrown in our direction from behind some bushes. Unfortunately, this act of caution did not occur to us at the beginning and it was not until near the end of our stay there that we realised how much our behaviour scandalised them; they called us heathens, Mohammedans and Jews; the latter being the worst of the epithets, according to them. The Mayor demonstrated his disapproval of us before his underlings; I suppose that the priest even took us for the subject of his sermons. The shirt and trousers my daughter wore also scandalised them. They considered it terrible that a young girl of nine years old should run about the mountain side *disguised as a man*. And it was not only the peasants who demonstrated this prudery.

On Sundays, a cornet sounded that could be heard throughout the town and the surrounding area, to remind laggards that it was the hour to perform their offices; it arrived at our ears in vain. We were deaf to it; at first because we did not understand its significance, and when we did understand, we were even deafer to it. In response, the villagers, to avenge this slight on the glory of God, took measures which were distinctly unchristian. They reached an agreement amongst themselves to sell us their fish, eggs and vegetables, only at an exorbitant price. They did not allow us to invoke a known price or custom. At the least disagreement, the peasant selling the goods, putting on proud Spanish airs, would state: "So, Madam doesn't want them, I take it." Then stuffing his onions, or potatoes back into his saddle-bags, would add: "In that case, you shall not have them!" and he would then retire majestically, without allowing for any possible bargaining. We were forced to fast, in penitence for having dared to haggle.

In fact we really did have to fast. There was neither competition, nor discounts to be had among the sellers.

The one who came afterwards would demand double and the third, three times as much; forcing us to live the life of anchorites at a price that would have paid for the life of a Prince in Paris. However, we did have recourse to supplies from Palma, via the cook of the French consul, who was our salvation; if I were an Emperor of Rome, I would have set his cotton cap among the constellations. However, on rainy days, no carrier would risk the roads at any price, and as it rained, in large part, for two months, we were often reduced to bread as hard as ship's biscuit, and we dined like real monks.

This would have been a trivial inconvenience, had we all been in good health. I am strong, sober, and even stoic by nature when it comes to eating. My children's splendid appetites led them to devour whatever was put on the table, and even a green lemon seemed to them a sweetmeat. My son, who had arrived in a weak and sickly condition, miraculously returned to full health, being cured of a most serious rheumatic condition, by running around the mountainside among the waist high wet grass, like a hare chased by hounds. Providence allowed nature to work wonders with him; and one invalid would have been enough.

However, the other, far from prospering in the damp air and the hardships, worsened to an alarming degree. Despite being condemned by all the doctors of Palma, he did not have a chronic illness: but the absence of a good fortifying diet, combined with a strong attack of catarrh, had left him in a lethargic state, from which he could not recover. He resigned himself to his Fate, as one can when the suffering is one's own, but we could not resign ourselves as easily to it as he, and for the first time, I experienced great worries over minor misfortunes. I would rage over a soup with too much pepper in it, or that had been dipped into by the pilfering serving girl, I grew anxious over fresh bread that did not arrive, or that had become spongy on fording a torrent in the saddlebags of a mule. I have no recollection of what I ate in Pisa or Trieste; but even if I live to be a hundred, I will never forget the arrival of baskets of provisions at the Charterhouse. What would I not have given for a consommé, and a glass of Bordeaux to offer to our invalid? Majorcan food, especially the way in which it was prepared, if we did not supervise its preparation, completely turned his stomach. Need I assert up to what point these worries were not groundless? One day we were served a meagre chicken, on whose steaming back we saw enormous fleas[4] leaping about, that Hoffman would have turned into evil spirits, but which he undoubtedly would not have appreciated in his sauce. My children suffered such a childish attack of laughter, that they nearly fell out of their chairs.

Majorcan cooking is almost solely based on pork, in all its forms, and all its aspects. It could perfectly well have been Majorca that the little Savoyard in the story was describing, when he said, in praise of his cheap

---

[4] The original has *Maîtres Floh* here, a pun on Hoffman's story *Herrenflöhe*. (The Flea Masters) [Tr. Note]

restaurant, that it sold five kinds of meat: hog, boar, swine, pig, bacon and ham. I am certain that Majorca boasts more than two thousand dishes prepared with pig meat, and at least two hundred different types of blood sausage, all seasoned with garlic, black and red pepper and all kinds of corrosive spices, which make every mouthful a health hazard. You will see appear before you on the table twenty dishes which appear good Christian fare, but do not be fooled, they are infernal concoctions, cooked by the Devil in person. Finally the dessert arrives, a good looking pie, with slices of fruit that appears to be candied orange; however it is a lard and garlic pie, with slices of *tomàtigues* (local tomatoes) and peppers, all sprinkled liberally with sea salt, that in your innocence you mistook for icing sugar. There are, of course, chickens, but they are all skin and bone. In Valldemosa, they would surely have added a tax of one *real* onto the price of every grain we gave them, to fatten them up. The fish they fetched us from the sea were very flat, and as dry as the chickens.

One day we bought a huge cuttlefish, for the pleasure of examining it. I have never seen an animal so repulsive. It had a body as big as a turkey, eyes as large as oranges, and flaccid, nauseous tentacles which, stretched out, measured four or five feet in length. The fishermen assured us that it was a delicacy. We were revolted by its appearance, and gave it to Maria Antonia, who prepared, and apparently enjoyed, it.

If our wonderment over the cuttlefish had brought

smiles to the locals' lips, it was our turn to laugh a few days later. Coming down the mountain, we saw the peasants leaving their work and hurtling down towards some people who had stopped on the path, and who carried a basket with a pair of admirable, extraordinary, marvellous, incomprehensible birds in it. The entire population of the mountain were stunned by the appearance of these unknown creatures. "What do they eat?" they asked, gaping at them. And someone responded:

"Maybe they don't eat!"

"Are they birds of the land or sea?"

"They probably spend all their time on the wing!"

Finally, when the two birds were about to be asphyxiated by the pressing crowd of admirers, we were able to verify that these were not condors, or phoenixes, or hippogryphs, but rather two beautiful farmyard geese, that a rich man was sending as a present to a friend of his.

In Majorca, as in Venice, wine based liqueurs are plentiful, and exquisite. Every day, we drank a muscatel as fine, and as inexpensive, as the Cyprian drank on the Adriatic coast. However, red wines, whose preparation is an art almost unknown among the Majorcans, were harsh, black, caustic, of a high alcohol content, and priced much higher than our cheapest French table-wine. These strong corrosive brews affected our invalid very badly, and ourselves also; so much so, that we usually drank the excellent local water. I do not know if the purity of that water was responsible or not, but we noticed that our teeth soon acquired a whiteness that no cosmetician in Paris would have been able to produce. However, our enforced abstemiousness may also have been partly responsible.

Not having access to butter, and not being able to stomach the fat, the nauseous oil, and the fumes from the indigenous cooking fires, we lived off lean meat, fish and vegetables, all seasoned with fresh spring water, to which we occasionally added, as a Sybaritic extravagance, the juice of a fresh orange recently picked from our garden. On the other hand, we did have superb desserts, sweet potatoes from Malaga, candied marrow from Valencia, and grapes worthy of the land of Canaan. These grapes, white or red, were elongated, and covered in a thick skin that helped keep them fresh throughout the entire year. They were splendid, and one could eat as many of them as one desired without experiencing that swelling of the stomach that our grapes produce. The grapes of Fontainebleau are more juicy and fresh, but those of Majorca are sweeter, and have more pulp. The latter can be eaten, but the former are best drunk. They come in bunches that can weigh up to twenty or twenty-five pounds, and would have caused admiration in a painter. They were our deliverance in times of hunger. The peasants thought they were selling them to us at a high price, forcing us to pay four times their market value; but they were unaware that, compared with the price of French grapes, they were still cheap, and so both sides had the luxury of imagining they had the last laugh. As for the prickly pears, we never bargained over them, they are without doubt the most detestable fruit I know.

As I have said, if the conditions of that frugal life had not been counterproductive, and even pernicious for one of us, the rest of us would have become accustomed to it. Even in Majorca, even in an abandoned monastery, even in conflict with the shrewdest peasants in the world, we had still managed to create a little pocket of wellbeing for ourselves. We had glass on the windows; doors, and a stove, a unique stove that had taken the best blacksmith in Palma a month to forge, and that had cost us a hundred francs. It was simply an iron cylinder with a pipe that stuck out of the window. It took a good hour to light, and as soon as it was lit, it became red hot, making it necessary to reopen the doors to allow the heat out; doors which had already previously been opened for a long time in order to let the smoke out. Besides, the blacksmith had covered the interior with a kind of mastic sealant made from a waste material that the Indians use to decorate the walls of their houses, and even their bodies; the cow, as is well-known, being a sacred animal for them. No matter how purifying for the soul that sacred odour might be, I can testify that it is not very delightful to the senses. In the month it took that mastic to dry, we imagined that we were in the circle of hell in which Dante had claimed to have seen the flatterers. I searched my memory in vain for a deed of that nature of which I could be said to be guilty; which Power had I lionized, which Pope or which King had I steered wrong through my obsequiousness? But in all conscience, I could not even find a doorman, or a bellhop, towards whom I had paid reverence, let alone a gendarme, or a journalist!

Luckily, the apothecary in the Charterhouse sold us some exquisite benzoic oil, which had been left over from the stock of perfumes with which incense had previously been made for the monastery church, to burn before the image of the Virgin; and that celestial emanation victoriously combated the exhalations from the eighth pit of hell in our cell.

The furniture we had was splendid, impeccable folding beds, mattresses that were a little too soft and more expensive than those of Paris, but new and clean, and large and excellent quilted counterpanes, sold quite cheaply by the Jews of Palma. A French lady, who had settled on the island, had the goodness to lend us several pounds of feathers she had brought from Marseilles, and with those we made two pillows for our invalid. That was surely a great luxury, in a place where geese were considered almost mythical beasts, and where chickens have to scratch themselves, even when they come out of the oven.

We had a number of tables, quite a few straw-seated chairs, like those you see in peasant cottages in our country, and also a voluptuous sofa in deal, with cushions stuffed with wool. The floor of the cell was uneven and dusty, and covered with long straw mats from Valencia, that made it look like a sun dried lawn, and we also had those beautiful long haired sheepskins of an admirable quality and whiteness, which are prepared very well on the island.

Like in Africat and Asia, there are few cupboards in the old houses on Majorca, so there were none at all in the Charterhouse. They store their effects in huge deal chests. Our light-coloured leather trunks would pass muster as elegant pieces of furniture there. A great colourful tartan shawl, which we used as a blanket during our trip, now became a sumptuous curtain hanging from the alcove, and my son decorated the stove with some of those charming clay urns from Felanitx, which in shape and decoration were distinctly Moorish.

Felanitx is a Majorcan village that should be given the task of supplying the whole of Europe with these fine-looking vases, which are so light you would think they were made of cork, and of a grain so fine, that the clay they are made of could be mistaken for some better-quality material. They make beautifully shaped small water jugs there, that they use to keep their water wonderfully cool. The clay is so porous, that the water eventually seeps out through the sides, and in only six hours they will empty. I am definitely no physicist, and perhaps my observation here is a little naïve; but it seemed marvellous to me, even magical perhaps, how we would leave our jug full of water on the stove, whose iron surface was nearly always red hot, and later when all the water had seeped out from the pores of the container, it would not crack open, despite being bone dry. While it still had a drop of water left in it, that drop would remain icy cold, even though the temperature of the stove was such that it scorched wood left on top of it. That pretty little vase, garnished with ivy, taken off the wall outside, was more pleasing to the eye of an artist than all of the gilded ceramics from our modern Sèvres.

The Pleyel Piano, which we finally managed to wheedle out of the hands of the customs officers, after three weeks wrangling and four hundred Francs of duty, filled the high arched ceiling with sound that resonated gloriously throughout the cell. Finally, the sacristan consented to have us brought a large impressive Gothic chair, in carved oak, that the rats and the worms had been nibbling in the ancient Charterhouse chapel. The frame of the chair made a good bookcase, whilst, of an evening, its lacy fretwork and its skeletal spires cast rich shadows upon the wall in the shimmer of the lamplight, helping to restore the medieval, monkish atmosphere of the cell.

Señor Gomez, our former landlord at *Son Vent*, the rich man who had furtively hired us his house, because it might have aroused comment if a citizen of Majorca was seen to be speculating with his property, caused quite a commotion when he threatened to take us to court for having broken some clay plates, that he charged us for as if they had been finest porcelain from China. He also made us pay, (also through threats), for the whitewashing and re-plastering of the entire house, measures he insisted he had to take to counter the contagion of our invalid's catarrh. However, every cloud has a silver lining; so anxious was he to rid himself of everything we might have touched, that he sold us all the household linen from the house we had hired, not without insisting on bargaining and ensuring we paid for them as if new. However, thanks to him, we were not forced to sow flax, so that one day we would be able to make ourselves sheets and tablecloths, like that Italian Lord who made a similar arrangement as regards the shirts of his peasants.

I hope my readers are not going to accuse me of childishness when I report irritations that, after all, did no more than cost me deep in the purse. I bear no resentments, but offer these incidents as interesting observations of the behaviour of people, because, after all, the most interesting factor in foreign travel is surely observing the conduct of other people. I never had a single relationship involving money, no matter how petty the amount, with the Majorcans, which did not reveal to me their shameless duplicity, and vulgar greed. If I add that they delighted in parading their piety before us, while pretending to be ever so offended by our lack of faith, my readers must surely agree that the piousness of simple souls, held up as exemplary by certain conservative elements in society today, hardly represents the most edifying and moral example in the world today. The reader will surely recognize, then, that I felt that we had the right to seek to comprehend and worship our creator in a way that we saw more fit. I have heard the argument many times that it is criminal and dangerous to undermine even a corrupted faith, when you have nothing to put in its place; that people who have not been contaminated by the poison of philosophical inquiry, or the frenzy of revolution, are the only true moralists, the only truly hospitable, and sincere people left; that they still have poetry, greatness and the ancient virtues, etc, etc. I am afraid that on Majorca I laughed at that argument, even more loudly than usual. When I saw my children, educated in the abomination and desolation of philosophy, minister to, and wait upon, a suffering friend with gladness in their hearts, they and they alone, amidst one hundred and sixty thousand Majorcans, who with harsh inhumanity, and cowardly terror, would have turned their backs on an invalid considered contagious, I told myself that the those little imps were more estimable and charitable than that entire population of saints and apostles.

Those pious servants of God never stopped telling me that I was committing a great crime in exposing my children to contagion, and that in punishment for my blindness, heaven would send them the same illness. I replied that in our family, if one of us had the plague, the others would not flee from their bedside; that it was not customary in pre-revolutionary, or post revolutionary, France, to abandon the sick to their fate; that certain Spanish prisoners, suffering from severe illnesses had crossed our territory, during the Napoleonic wars, and that our peasants, after having shared with them their food bowl, and their linen, had granted them beds to sleep in, and had remained by their sides to comfort them, that several had been victims of this charity and had succumbed to the contagion, but that this had not stopped the rest from exercising hospitality and charity. The Majorcan, in reply, would shake his head, and smile condescendingly; the idea of sacrificing their lives for a stranger being as alien a concept to them as that of being straightforward, and even friendly, towards a foreigner.

Visitors to the interior of the island have marvelled at the hospitality and unselfishness of the Majorcan farmer. They have written with admiration that, although the country has few inns, it was still easy and pleasing to travel about the country, because a *simple recommendation* was enough to ensure the traveller was received, accommodated, and treated as an honoured guest, without charge. This simple recommendation seems to me to be the key here. These travellers omitted to mention that all of the classes on Majorca, and therefore all of the inhabitants, maintain a commonality of interests that leads to sociable relationships between themselves, but in which religious charity, and human sympathy, play very little part. A few words will explain this pecuniary situation.

The nobility are rich in property, but poor in rents, and ruined by mortgages. The Jews, who are numerous, are rich in ready money, and have all of the properties of the aristocracy in their holding, so that it could be said that the island belongs to them. Thus, the nobility do little more than play at being Lords of their Dominions and Palaces, for the benefit of themselves, and the few foreigners who occasionally visit the island. In order to play their role to the hilt, they are forced to take out further loans from the Jews every year, and the snowball grows larger, annually. I have already mentioned earlier just how stagnant commerce is on the island, due to the lack of merchandise and industry; however, it is a point of honour for those gentlemen to accept their ruin slowly and placidly, without denying themselves the least luxury, just as their prodigal forefathers did in their time. The speculators then are in an enduring commonality of interests with the farmers, from whom they receive part of their rents, in virtue of the titles conceded to them by the aristocracy.

Thus the peasant, who perhaps benefits by this division of his debts, pays his Lord as little as possible, and the banker as much as he can. His lord is dependent and resigned; the Jew, inexorable, but patient. The Jew makes concessions, affects great tolerance, and allows time, while pursuing his aim, with diabolic genius. Once he has his claws into a property, it is only a matter of time before, piece by piece, it all ends up in his hands, and it is in his interest to make himself indispensable until the debt reaches the value of the capital. Within twenty years, there will be no aristocrat on Majorca, and the Jews will establish themselves in power, as they have done among us and raise their heads, now still lowered in hypocritical humility beneath the badly dissimulated disdain of the nobility, and the impotence and childlike revulsion of the proletariat. Meanwhile, they remain the true owners of the lands, and the peasant trembles before them; the peasant, who turns his eyes painfully towards his former lord, and weeps with tenderness, while taking the last scraps of the ancient fortune for himself. In short, he needs to try and satisfy both masters, for fear of being crushed between them both.

You must arrive then with a letter of recommendation addressed to some peasant from a nobleman, or someone rich (who else could recommend you, since there is no middle-class on the island), and instantly the doors will open for you. But try and ask for a glass of water from a peasant without such a recommendation, and you will see what happens.

Yet despite all of this, the Majorcan peasant is kind, considerate, peaceful in his ways, and naturally calm and patient. He loves not evil, but he knows not good. He confesses, prays, is obsessed with attaining a place in heaven, but ignores the true duties of a member of the human race. He is no more worthy of hate than an ox or a sheep, but is not much more of a man than the insensible being within the innocent brute. He says his prayers like a superstitious savage, but he would eat his fellow citizen without compunction, if that was the custom of the land, and if he did not have enough pork to hand. He does not consider the foreigner a human being, so he will cheat him, make him pay over the odds, lie to him, insult him and pilfer from him without the least scruple. He would never even steal an olive from his neighbour; but to the Majorcan way of thinking, the mass of humanity living beyond the sea only exist in God's plan to generate a little income for the islanders.

We had nicknamed Majorca *Monkey Island* because, being surrounded by those cunning, robbing and yet innocent beasts, we had become accustomed to defending ourselves from them, with no more malice or spite than that which the Indian feels towards the mischievous monkeys or orang-utans that besiege him.

However, one cannot become accustomed, without a certain sadness, to seeing creatures in apparently human form, ostensibly touched by the Divine Hand, vegetating in a land that is so far from the mainstream of human progress. One can see that this imperfect being is capable of understanding, that his race is perfectible, that in the future he will share the fate of the more advanced races, and that this can only be a matter of time; which although it might appear long to us, is truly inappreciable within the abyss of eternity. However, the more one sees the potential in these beings, the more one suffers to see them repressed by the chains of the past. Although this waiting period does not appear to worry Providence, it terrifies and distresses our short-lived existences. We feel it in our hearts, in our souls, in our innermost parts, that the lives of others are linked to ours, that we have no choice but to love or be loved, to understand and be understood, to aid and to be assisted. A sense of moral and intellectual superiority over others can only gratify the proud. I imagine that the wish of any open hearted person would not be to want to drag themselves down to the level of the lowest, but that, in a wink of an eye, they could raise up those below them in society to their own level, so they could truly live, at last, a life of compassion, of colloquy, equality and community, which is the ideal behind all of the religions that have sprung from the human conscience.

I am sure that this need is to be found in the bottom of every heart, and that those who fight against it, believing they have stifled it out of themselves with fallacious arguments, suffer a strange, bitterness, which they find difficult to put a name to. The people from the lower classes tire themselves out, or fade away, when they cannot rise from their misery; those at the top become indignant or impatient at ineffectually offering a helping hand; while those who have no thought of helping anyone, are devoured by world-weariness and the dread of solitude, until they fall themselves into a stultification that makes their lives even shoddier than those at the lowest depths.

CHAPTER FOUR

e were alone, then, on Majorca, as alone as if we were in the middle of a desert; and when our daily bread was attained by fighting for it with the *monkeys*, we would sit together as a family, huddled around the stove, and laugh at it all. However, as winter advanced, sadness paralysed any efforts towards joy and serenity in my breast. The state of health of our invalid grew steadily worse every day; the wind howled along the watercourse of the stream, the wind shook our windows, thunder shook our thick walls, and interrupted the children's laughter and play with its sombre rumble. Eagles and vultures, emboldened by the sea mist,

plunged down to attack and eat our poor little birds, even right out of the pomegranate tree that grew in front of my window. The enraged sea kept all the boats in port; we felt like prisoners, far from all enlightened help, and all effective sympathy. Death seemed to hover over our heads, seeking to take possession of one of us, and we were the only ones who opposed his designs on his prey. There was not a single human creature within reach who did not wish to hurry him to his grave, so as to end more quickly the perceived peril of his proximity. The thought of this hostility was horrendously gloomy. Fortunately, we felt sufficiently strong and selfless to take turns at ministering to our patient, and thus compensate for the assistance and sympathy they denied us. In fact, I believe that in such difficulties, the heart grows stronger, and is bolstered by the revitalizing effect of human solidarity. However, we suffered in our souls to find ourselves cast among beings who could not understand this sentiment, and for whom we ended up feeling the deepest pity, rather than receiving from them a morsel of sympathy.

I also felt great unease. I have no scientific knowledge whatsoever, and we needed a doctor, a great doctor, to cure our invalid's illness, the entire responsibility for which weighed heavily on my heart.

I do not doubt the ability, or the zeal, of the doctor who came to see us, but he was wrong in his diagnosis, a mistake which any doctor, even the most illustrious, can make. As he himself confessed, any professional can, and does, make mistakes frequently. Our invalid's bronchitis had given way to a nervous condition that produced several of the symptoms associated with consumptive laryngitis. The doctor, who had witnessed these symptoms at certain moments, and who had not witnessed anything to the contrary, which I had observed while watching over the patient at other times, pronounced in favour of a regime appropriate for consumptives: bleeding, and a strict milk based diet. These measures were completely counter-productive, and the bleeding would have been fatal. The invalid sensed this by instinct, and I, while no physician, have cared for many sick people, and I also perceived this. However, I shuddered at the idea of trusting in my instincts, which could have been deceiving me, and struggling against the advice of a professional. When I saw our invalid getting worse, I suffered real anxieties that anyone might comprehend. "Bleeding will save him", I was told. "And if you deny him this, he will die." Yet my inner voice told me in my dreams: "Bleeding will kill him, and if you prevent it happening you will save his life." I am persuaded that this voice was that of Providence and now that our friend, the terror of the Majorcans, is seen to be no more consumptive than I am, I thank heaven for giving me the confidence to trust in the instincts that saved him.

The recommended diet was not to his taste at all. When we saw the negative effects of it, we followed it as little as possible, but unfortunately there was not a lot of choice, it was either the hot spices of the island, or the frugal diet. Milk products, whose pernicious effects we were to recognise later, were luckily not common on Majorca, which does not produce any. At that time we still believed that milk worked wonders, and we exerted ourselves to obtain it. There are no cows in those mountains, and the goat's milk we ordered was often half drunk by the children who brought it, though that did not prevent it from arriving as full as when it left the goatherds'. It was a miracle that took place every morning when the pious messenger boy stopped to pray in the Charterhouse patio, right next to the water fountain. To put a stop to these prodigious events, we procured a goat. She was the sweetest and most adorable creature in the world, a beautiful chamois coloured, short-haired, hornless, African nanny goat, with a hooked nose, and long floppy ears. These animals are so different from ours. They have the coat of a goat, and the profile of a sheep, but they do not have the mischievous, puckish physiognomy of our kids. In fact they seem full of melancholy. They are also different from our goats, in having smaller udders that yield considerably less milk. When they are mature, their milk has a harsh, savage taste that the Majorcans seem to value, but which was repugnant to us.

Our little friend at the Charterhouse was in her first maternity; she was not yet two years old, and her milk was especially smooth, but she was very miserly with it, above all when separated from the herd she was accustomed, not to gambol with (she was far too serious, too Majorcan, for that), but rather to ruminate on top of the mountain with. Separated from her companions, she fell into a kind of depression, which was comparable to ours. Although we had good grass in our patio, and good herbs, cultivated, until recently by the monks, which still grew in the irrigation ditches, nothing would reconcile her to her captivity. She wandered through the cloisters, confused and distressed, bleating so disconsolately that it was a wonder the stone walls did not crack at the sound. To keep her company, we bought a fat sheep with thick white shaggy fleece, some six inches long, one of those sheep that in France one only sees these days in the window of a toy shop, or on our grandmothers' fans. This excellent companion restored our kid's composure, somewhat, and also yielded us a creamy milk herself. However, between the two of them, and despite being well-fed, they gave us so little milk, that we soon began to suspect the frequent visits to the animals of Maria Antonia, *la niña* and Catalina. So we put them under lock and key in a little courtyard at the foot of the bell tower, and took it upon ourselves to milk them. That thin milk, mixed with the milk of almonds, which my children and I took turns in squeezing out of the nuts, made a healthy and pleasant medicinal beverage. There was little chance of obtaining any other medicines. All the drugs available in Palma were intolerably dirty. The sugar, imported from Spain, was badly refined, dark, and oily, and had purgative powers for those not accustomed to it.

One day we thought we were saved, because we saw violets growing in the garden of a wealthy farmer. He allowed us to pick them to make an infusion, and when we had made our little packet up he charged us a sou a violet, a Majorcan sou, which was worth three French sous.

In addition to these familial anxieties, we had to sweep the rooms, and make the beds ourselves when we wished to sleep at night; because the Majorcan maid could not touch anything without passing on to us, in great prodigiousness, the same visitors my children had been so amused at finding on the back of a steaming chicken. We hardly had any time left for work and walks, but those hours were indeed well spent. The children listened attentively to their lessons, and then we only had to poke our noses out of from our den to find ourselves in the most varied, and delightful landscape. Framed by the surrounding mountains, each step took us to some fortuitously picturesque scene, a tiny chapel, balanced on a cliff edge, a little wood of strawberry trees[1], nestling on the side of a craggy slope, a hermitage, next to a spring full of tall reeds, a coppice of trees, perched on huge moss-covered rocks enveloped in ivy. When the sun deigned to show its face for a moment, all of the plants, rocks, and rain-washed terrain would become resplendent in colour, with highlights of incredible brilliance.

---

[1] The original has *rosage*, the Laureum Rose, (Rhododendron ferrugineux), but the author was surely mistaken in this identification, as that is an Alpine plant. I have substituted a more probable candidate: the Strawberry Tree, (arbutos unedo), which bears a passing resemblance to the other, but which produces fruit resembling strawberries, in late autumn. It grows abundantly in just the type of landscape she describes. (TR. Note)

Two of our walks were particularly worthy of note. However, the memory of the first (which we took towards the beginning of our stay on Majorca), is rather painful for me because our companion, who was in good health at the time, had insisted on accompanying us to share the magnificent views, and I believe it was the exertion of that walk which brought on his illness.

Our objective was a hermitage on the coast, some three miles from the Charterhouse. We followed the right flank of the mountain range, and climbed up from hill to hill following a rock-strewn path that was hard on the feet, until we reached the northern coast of the island. At every bend on the way, we had a fine view out across a carpet of lush vegetation towards the sea far below us. It was the first time I had seen a fertile coastline, covered in trees and vegetation, right down to the first waves; no white cliffs, no desolate stretches of sand, no muddy beaches. Along the entire French coast that I have seen, even at the heights of Port-Vendres, where all of its spectacular beauty opened out before me, the sea had always seemed to me dirty or unpleasant to approach. The highly praised Venice Lido has terrifyingly bare sands, populated by enormous lizards that suddenly scurry beneath your feet in their thousands, and seem to follow you in ever increasing numbers, like in some nightmare. At Royant, in Marseilles, in fact, almost everywhere along our coasts, I believe, there is a belt of sterile sand, and a line of viscous seaweed that presents a barrier hindering all access to the sea. In Majorca, I saw the sea as I had always dreamed of her, clear and blue as the sky, gently rolling like a sapphire plain, ploughed into furrows, whose movement at a distance was difficult to appreciate, and framed by forests of the deepest green. Each step we took along that sinuous mountain path offered us a new panorama, more sublime than the previous one. Nonetheless, to reach the hermitage we had to descend a lot to reach the shoreline, which, although beautiful at that point, did not possess the grandiose splendour that I would find in another part of the coast some months later.

The four or five hermits who lived there lacked anything of poetry. Their dwelling was as wretched, and rough, as one could imagine a hermitage being. From their terraced vegetable garden, where we surprised them digging, only the solitude of the sea stretches out before their eyes. They wore no religious habits, and they seemed to us to be the stupidest recluses in the world. Their prior put down his spade, and came over to us in a loose-fitting, beige-coloured jacket; with his short hair and dirty beard, he was far from picturesque. He talked to us of the harshness of their lives, and above all of the intolerable cold that held sway over that coast; but when we asked him if it ever froze, our combined efforts failed to communicate to him what frost was. He did not recognise the word in any language, and had never heard tell of lands which were colder than Majorca. However, he did have certain notions about France because he had seen the French fleet pass by in 1830, on its way to conquer Algiers; this had been the most dramatic, most astonishing and, perhaps, the only spectacle in his life. He asked us if the French had managed to take Algiers and when we told him the French had recently captured Constantine, his eyes opened as wide as saucers, and he exclaimed that the French were indeed a great people.

He took us up to an incredibly dirty cell, where we saw the chief hermit. We took him for a centenarian, and were quite shocked to learn that he was only eighty. He was in a perfect state of imbecility, although he still mechanically made wooden spoons with shaking, earthy hands. Although not deaf, he paid us scant attention, until the prior called out to him, whereupon he turned his enormous head towards us, which I would have sworn was made of wax, and revealed a hideously stultified face. There was an entire life of intellectual debasement revealed in that decomposed countenance, and I had to hastily avert my eyes from one of the most upsetting and piteous sights in the world. We gave them alms, as they were of a mendicant order that is still venerated by the peasants, who will not allow them to want for anything.

On our return to the Charterhouse, we were assailed by a violent wind that blew us over several times, and which made our progress so exhausting that our invalid was fatigued by the exertion.

The second noteworthy walk we took some days before we left Majorca, and it caused such an effect on me that I shall never forget it as long as I live. A sight of natural beauty had never before made such an impact on me, nor left such a lasting impression. In fact, I believe that I have had an experience like it but three or four times, in my entire life.

The rains had ceased at last, and suddenly it was spring. It was now February; all the almond trees had come into blossom, and the meadows were filled with heady scented jonquils. Apart from the colour of the sky, and the vivacity of the tones in the landscape, this was the only perceptible difference between the two seasons; because the majority of trees in the area are evergreens. Here, trees that bud early do not have to face a biting frost; the grasses maintain all of their freshness, and the flowers only need one morning of sun to decide to show their faces. When our garden was under six inches of snow, there were still climbing roses clinging to the trellises, being blown about in the gusts of wind, and although they seemed paler than usual, they still endured the conditions with apparent good humour.

I often looked out towards the north and the sea from the monastery gate and one day, when our invalid was sufficiently comfortable to be able to remain alone for two or three hours, we finally set out in that direction to view that coast. Up to that moment, I had not the least curiosity about it, despite the fact that my children, who had romped all over the area like mountain goats, had assured me that it was the most beautiful place in the world. Perhaps my visit to the hermitage, and its baleful consequences, had left me with a justifiable resentment, or perhaps I simply did not expect much from a view at sea-level, that I suspected could not possibly be as magnificent as the view from the mountains. Whatever the reason, this was the first time that I had been tempted to venture out of the seclusion of the confines of the Valldemosa valley.

I have noted above that the Charterhouse straddles the mountain range, and that there is a gently sloping plain that rises up one flank separating us from the sea. Every day, I had glanced towards the sea on the horizon, far below this plain, and my vision and my reason had committed a singular error: instead of appreciating that this plain sloped up, and then ended a short distance away, I imagined that it gradually sloped down, to a shore some five or six leagues away. How can I explain then that this sea, which I had erroneously thought was on the same level as the Charterhouse, was in fact two or three thousand feet lower down? I had often been astounded to hear the sea so loud, being, as I had supposed, so far off, and I could offer no explanation for this phenomenon. I had not realised my mistake, and therefore I do not know why I allow myself to mock the Parisian bourgeoisie so often, when my own conjectures are frequently so wide of the mark. I had not appreciated that the maritime horizon, on which I used to cast my gaze, was actually some fifteen or twenty leagues distant, while the sea which pounded the nearest point on the coast was a mere half an hour's walk away. Whenever my children had encouraged me to come and see the sea, claiming it was only a few paces away, I never seemed to

247

find the time, believing that what may have only been a couple of paces for a child, would in fact turn out to be giant's steps, for who is not aware that children walk with their imaginations, rather than their feet. The seven-league boots of Tom Thumb symbolically represent the idea that a child could circumnavigate the globe without fully realising the magnitude of what they had just done.

Finally, I let myself be persuaded by them, certain that we would never arrive at this illusory coast, which I considered so far off. My son claimed to know the way, but as every way is on the way when you are wearing seven league boots, and as for a long time now I have restricted my footwear to a pair of slippers, I objected that I could not follow him and his sister as they skipped over hedges, ditches and ravines. After a quarter of an hour I perceived that we were not descending towards the sea, since the streams ran swiftly towards us, and the further we went on, the farther away the sea appeared to recede into the horizon. I was convinced we should turn back, and determined to ask the first passing peasant if there was indeed any way we could chance upon the sea following this route.

Under a cluster of willow trees, in a muddy gully we came upon three shepherdesses, or perhaps they were witches[2] in disguise, who were digging in the mire for who knows what talisman, or what secret herb. The first of

---

[2] The original has *fairies*, but in English the word fairy brings to mind Tinker Bell and playful imps flitting about glades. The associations of the word in French are far darker and more shadowy. (Tr. Note)

them only had a single tooth; she was probably the witch *Dentue*, who stirs her spells in a cauldron, using this solitary and horrible tooth. The second old crone was, to judge by appearances, *Carabosse*, the most mortal enemy of orthopaedic establishments. Both of them gave us a horrible grimace. Then the first of them advanced her terrible tooth in the direction of my daughter, whose freshness must have quickened her appetite. The second lifted her head, and brandished her crutch as if about to thrash my son's loins in punishment for the offence his straight and slim figure must have seemed to her. But the third, who was young and pretty, gracefully sprang out of the ditch and, casting her cloak over her shoulder, she gestured towards us with her hand, and started walking off in front of us. She was surely a good witch, but, disguised as a mountain girl, she preferred to go by the name of *Perica de Pier-Bruno*.

Perica was the most delightful creature I saw in Majorca. She, and our goat, are the only living things who still keep a piece of my heart in Valldemosa. Still, had our goat been covered in as much mud as this young country lass, it would have blushed. However, a short walk through the damp grass soon returned the colour to her bare feet, which were not exactly white, but an appealing olive shade like an Andalusian. Her smile, her confident, curious chatter and her unselfish readiness to oblige, made us feel that we had stumbled upon a priceless pearl. She was sixteen, and had the most delicate features, with a face as rounded and velvety as a peach. She had a figure as pure in line and as beautifully symmetrical as a Greek statue. Her waist was as thin as a reed, and her bare arms were tanned a light sienna. Her hair tumbled out from beneath her coarse linen *rebosillo*, as flowing and tangled as a young mare's tail. She led us to the edge of her field, then through a sowed meadow surrounded by trees and huge boulders. The sea was now no longer in sight, and I began to think that she was playing a trick on us, and we were being led up the mountain path.

Suddenly, however, she opened a gate that closed off the meadow, and we saw a path that wound past a huge rock in the form of a sugar loaf. We followed the path, and then, as if by magic, we found ourselves suddenly high above the sea, with an abyss between us and the shore, a league beneath our feet. This unexpected sight gave me vertigo at first, and I was forced to sit down. Little by little, I calmed down, and regained enough confidence to continue down the path, although it was far more suited to the hooves of goats, than the feet of human beings. The view was so fabulous, that I no longer had seven league boots on, but rather swallow's wings; and I glided around the tall limestone pinnacles that stood like hundred foot high giants along the rock face of the coast, always trying to glimpse the base of the cove that disappeared amidst the depths to my right, down where the fishing boats seemed no bigger than flies.

Suddenly, I saw nothing in front of me, or below me, at all, but the blue of the sea. The path had wandered off, I know not where. Perica was shouting above my head, and the children, who had been following me on all fours, had begun screaming. I turned around and saw my daughter crying, and then retraced my footsteps to see what the matter was. When I had had time to think, I began to grasp that the children's terror and desperation was not unfounded. One step more, and I might have been descending considerably faster than I had planned, unless I had been able to hang upside down, like a fly on the ceiling, because the rocks I had been climbing along jutted out over the little bay, and the base of the cliffs was considerably more eroded than the upper reaches. When I realised the danger I had been leading my children into, I felt great fear and I felt compelled to climb back up with them. However, when I had left them in a place where they were safe, behind one of the gigantic sugar loaves, the obsession with seeing the bottom of the cove, and the underside of these overhangs, once more possessed me.

I guessed that I would never have seen anything remotely resembling the spectacle waiting to present itself before my eyes, and my imagination began to race. I descended on another path, clinging to the shrubs and hugging the stone sides of the pinnacles, each one of which marked another sudden descent. Finally, I began to distinguish the immense hollow at the base of the cliffs into which the waves dashed with a strange musical sound. I thought I heard magical chords on the air, and I felt gratified that I had discovered who knows what unknown world. Then abruptly, my son, frightened and angry, appeared beside me, and began to tug energetically at my skirts to pull me back. I could not help falling in the least poetic way possible, not forwards, which would have been the end of my adventure, and of me, but rather, like any sensible person, backwards, as I sat down in a heap. My son gave me such a scolding, that I abandoned my enterprise, but not without a disappointment that still haunts me; because every year my slippers are getting heavier, and I do not think that I will ever re-grow the wings I had that day, to take me down onto shores such as those.

Nevertheless, it is undeniable, and I know it as well as the next person, that what you witness is not always equal to what you envisioned. However, this is only completely accurate in the arts, and the works of men. Whether it is because I have a limited imagination, or because God has much more talent than I (which is quite possible), I have usually found Nature to be infinitely more beautiful than how I had imagined it, and I do not remember having found anything in it of a disagreeable nature, unless I myself was feeling that way on the day.

Consequently, I will never reconcile myself to not having rounded that next rock. Perhaps I would have seen Amphitrite herself, stood under an arch of mother-of-pearl, her forehead crowned with rustling seaweed. Instead of which, all I saw was limestone pinnacles, some, thrusting out of the cliff face like columns, others, hanging down like stalactites in a cave, and assuming strange shapes, and fantastical postures. Then there were the incredibly hardy trees, twisted and half uprooted by the wind, leaning out over the abyss; and in the depths of that abyss another mountain, rising vertically out of the sea, a mountain of crystal, diamond, or sapphire; that in fact was the sea, which seen from a considerable height, produces the illusion, which most people have experienced, of being a vertical plane. Explain that, whoever can.

My children then decided that they wanted to collect some plants. Among those cliffs grow the most beautiful liliaceous plants in the world. Between the three of us we finally managed to uproot a bulb of *amaryllis escarlata*, which we did not take back to the Charterhouse, in the end, because it weighed too much. My son cut that marvellous plant up into pieces to take back a section, as big as his head, to show our invalid. Perica, loaded down with a huge bundle of firewood which she had been collecting along the way, and which her frequent brusque movements thrust into our faces, returned us to the outskirts of the village. I insisted she came into the Charterhouse, so as to give her a small token of our gratitude, but it took us a great effort before she agreed to accept it. Poor Perica, you will never know how much good you did my heart showing me that among those monkeys there was such a sweet human creature, so charming and obliging, and with no ulterior motives! That night we were so happy that we had not left Valldemosa without having found such a wonderful person.

CHAPTER FIVE

etween our two walks, the first and the last we took on Majorca, we had taken many that I will not recall here, for fear of boring the reader with my monotonous enthusiasm for the natural beauty to be found everywhere on the island, where features such as cottages, shacks, palaces, churches, and monasteries compete with one another for the honour of being the most picturesque object. However, should one of our grand painters ever decide to visit Majorca one day, I would recommend that he visit the country house called the *Granja de Fortuny*, with its little valley full of orange-trees that opens out beyond its marble

colonnades, along with the entire path that leads up to it. However, even without going all the way out to there, he could not take ten paces on this enchanted island, without stopping at every bend of the path to admire a Moorish water trough in the shade of some palm trees, or reflect upon a delicately worked 15th century stone cross, or gaze across a field of olive trees.

Nothing is equal to the strange power and beauty of the forms of these Majorcan olive trees. The locals claim that the most recent plantation was sown at the time of the Roman occupation. A fact that I will not question, since I do not know of any way of scientifically contesting the claim, even if I wished to do so, which thought has never entered my head. Seeing their remarkable contours, their vast trunks, and the gnarled aspect of these mysterious trees, my imagination willingly takes them for contemporaries of Hannibal. Whenever we walked among them at dusk, we had to keep reminding ourselves that they were trees, since, if we trusted to our eyes and our imaginations, we would have been terrified among those fantastical creatures, some twisting towards us like enormous dragons, with their mouths wide open and their wings unfolded, others coiled up like sleeping boa constrictors, others frantically clasping at each other like wrestlers seeking a winning hold. There rises a centaur at the gallop, with some hideous she-monkey on his back, there lies an unidentifiable reptile, devouring a whimpering doe, over there is a satyr, dancing with a billy goat a little less ugly than he; or often it is only a single, hollow, knotty, twisted, and misshapen tree, that we took for ten separate trees, and which appears to represent all of these different monsters in a single head as horrible as those multi-faceted Indian fetishes, and crowned with a single green branch for a crest. The curious reader, who turns over the pages of M. Lauren's illustrations, can rest assured that he has not exaggerated the physiognomy of the olive trees he has drawn. He could have chosen even more extraordinary specimens, and I hope that the *Magasin Pittoresque*, that amusing and indefatigable vulgarizer of the marvels of art and nature, will take pains to visit the island one of these days, to show us some of the most curious examples.

However, in order to represent, in great style, those sacred trees, from which one is always expecting to hear prophetic voices emerge, and the brilliant sky, against which one distinguishes their jagged silhouette, it would be necessary to seek the bold and glorious paintbrush of Theodore Rousseau.[1] The clear waters in which are mirrored asphodels and myrtles would need a Dupré.[2] Other, more formal, scenery, where Nature, although undomesticated, appears to have adopted a proud, classical air through sheer coquetry, would perhaps

---

[1] Rousseau, one of the best landscape painters of our times, is virtually unknown to the public at large due to the obstinacy of the selection committee at the Paris Salon, who have prevented him exhibiting his masterpieces for years. (Author's Note)
Not to be confused with Henri Rousseau; Theodore (1812-1867) helped found the Barbizon school of landscape painters, whose most famous affiliate was Millet. (Tr. Note)

[2] Jules Dupré (1811 - 1889) another painter of the Barbizon school. (Tr. Note)

tempt the more serious Corot[3]. However, in order to be able to express the delightful scrubland, with its profusion of grasses, wild flowers, old tree trunks, and weeping garlands over the mysterious spring into which storks wade their long legs, I would need the burin of Huet[4], like some magic wand, at my disposal.

Many times I have seen an aging Majorcan gentleman, standing at the threshold of his yellowing, half-ruined palace and immediately thought of Decamps[5], the grand master who raised caricature to the level of historical painting, the man of genius who knew how to give spirit, joy and poetry, in a word: life, even to a few walls! The beautiful brown-skinned children who played in our cloister, dressed as monks, would have greatly amused him. He would have added monkeys to the scene, and angels among the monkeys, pigs with human faces, and cherubim mixed among the pigs, and no less dirty; he would have put Perica, as beautiful as Galatea, encrusted in mud, like a hunting hound, and laughing in the sunshine, like everything that is beautiful on the face of the earth.

But it is you dearest Eugene[6], my old friend and dearest artist, who I would like to have taken up the

---

[3] Camille (Jean-Baptiste) Corot (1796-1875). Landscape painter and precursor to the impressionists. (Tr. Note)

[4] Paul Huet. Landscape painter associated with the Romantic School and influenced by Constable. (Tr. Note)

[5] Alexander Decamps (1803-1860) another leading light of the Barbizon school. (Tr. Note)

[6] Eugene Delacroix, (1798-1863), considered the greatest French Romantic painter. (Tr. Note)

mountain that night, when the moon illuminated the deathly pale floodplain.

The landscape was lovely, but I and my fourteen year old son were nearly drowned there. However, he never lost courage, and I never lost the ability to appreciate the beauty of nature that showed itself supremely romantic, supremely crazy, and yet totally awe-inspiring on this occasion.

My son and I had left Valldemosa in the middle of the winter rainy season, to go and continue our fight for the Pleyel piano with the malicious customs officials of Palma. The morning had been quite clear, and the paths were negotiable; but while we were walking around the city, it began to rain cats and dogs. In France, we complain about rain, but we do not really know what it is; our longest downpours last less than two hours; the clouds come close on each others heels, but there is usually a brief break in-between. In Majorca, a permanent blanket of cloud can envelop the island, and the rain can teem down until the last drop has fallen, which can take forty or fifty hours, or even four or five days without a break, and without any slackening of intensity.

Towards sunset, we returned to our coach, expecting to be back in the Charterhouse about three hours later. We took seven hours, and at one point we were about to spend the night with the frogs in an improvised lake. The driver of the *birlotxo* was in a foul mood, he had presented us with a thousand excuses for not departing; a horse needed shoeing, a mule was lame, an axle was broken, and I know not what else! However, by then, we had got to know the Majorcans well enough to not be fobbed off, and we insisted that he get up onto his position, from where he scowled most miserably for the first few hours. He did not sing; he did not accept our cigars; he did not even shout curses at the mule, which was a very bad sign; he had death in his soul. Wanting to terrify us, he had chosen the worst of the seven possible roads he knew. As this road descended quite a lot, we soon found ourselves driving through a torrent. The stream had broken its banks, left its usual course, and invaded the road, which was now no longer a carriage way, but rather a river, whose turbulent waters thundered towards us at great speed.

When the malicious coachman realised that we were not so pusillanimous, and that our resolve had not been shattered, he lost his composure, and started shouting oaths and curses that would crack the vault of the heavens. The carved stone conduits that carried spring water to the city had grown so full that they had burst, like the frog in the fable. Then, not knowing which direction to take, the liberated waters had formed pools, and then ponds, and then lakes, and finally a branch of the sea, in the middle of the countryside. After a short time, the coachman had run out of saints to call on for aid, or devils to offer his soul to. His legs were saturated, which was little less than he deserved, and we showed little sympathy towards him. The carriage was quite watertight, so we were still reasonably dry; but every second *the tide was rising*, as my son put it. We plunged on haphazardly, being jolted dreadfully, and plummeting into potholes, each one threatening to become our watery grave. Finally, we leaned over so much that the mule stopped, as if to compose himself to face his maker; the coachman dismounted and scrambled up the head-high bank at the side of the road; then he stopped, realising, by the crepuscular light, that this was in fact one side of the Valldemosa canal, which had been transformed into a river, that in sections gushed over its banks into our path, itself converted into a river lower down.

It was a tragic-comic moment. I was a little afraid for myself, and greatly afeared for my son. I looked over at him, and saw him laughing at the state of the coachman, who was standing, legs separated over his seat, looking down and estimating the depth of the abyss, now without the least desire to have his fun at our expense. When I saw my son so calm and amused, I recovered my faith in God. I felt that my child had within him a sense of his destiny, and I relied on that sixth sense that children cannot express, but that surrounds them like a cloud, or like a halo of sunbeams on their forehead.

The coachman, seeing that there was no way to abandon us to our doom, resigned himself to sharing it, and suddenly became all heroic, shouting out in a paternal voice: "Have no fear, my children!" Then he gave a great shout, lashed his mule, which tripped, slipped, got back up, tripped again, and finally, half-drowned, managed to move forward again. The carriage leaned perilously to one side; "This time!" came a cry; then over to the other. "No, this time!" was followed by sinister creaks, astonishing jerks, and lurches, and then finally we got back on course, like a ship that has been dashed against the rocks, but is lifted off by the next wave without breaking up.

We appeared saved, we were still dry; but there were several more rescues from being shipwrecked, before we managed to arrive at the mountain. Finally, we reached the ramp, but our mule, exhausted and terrified by the noise of the roaring torrent and the howling wind on the mountain, began to back up towards the precipice. We descended from the carriage to each push at a wheel, while the coachman pulled at the mule by his long ears. We repeated this manoeuvre, I do not know how many times; but after a two hour climb, we had not advanced even half a league. Then, when the mule, shuddering in every limb, refused once again to go forward over a bridge, we decided to abandon the man, his coach and his beast, and finish the journey to the monastery on foot.

This was no easy task. The quickest path had become a reckless torrent, against whose current one had to fight with all the strength of one's legs. Other impromptu torrents, cascading from the cliff tops with a great roar, often crossed our path to the right, forcing us to ford them with great danger, or attempt to leap across them before they became impassable. It rained oceans; great black clouds, darker than ink, frequently hid the face of the moon from our sight. Then, enveloped in that impenetrable greyish darkness, bent double by great gusts of wind, seeing the treetops bowed over almost to our head height, hearing the creaking of the fir trees, and feeling the stones rolling past our heels, we were forced to stop, and await for Jupiter to restore the light, as the poet says.

In the intervals of light and shadow, Eugene, you would have seen the sky and the earth dim and brighten successively, with the most sinister and outlandish effects of shadow and reflection. Whenever the wind created a clearing in the clouds, and the moon managed to penetrate the gloom to re-establish her reign over the deep-blue world, the wind would blow more clouds across her face; sombre clouds like fervent spectres, eager to blot out the lunar light with their shrouds. They would cloak her in their mantle, but then would part again to reveal her, more beautiful and accommodating than ever. Then the mountain, gushing forth in cascades, and the uprooted trees, would give us a glimpse of chaos. We thought of that astonishing witches' coven you had seen in some half-forgotten nightmare, and which you painted with a paintbrush dipped in the red and blue waves of Phlegethon and Erebus. No sooner had that infernal scene formed before our eyes, than it disappeared, as the moon was devoured by those monsters of the air, and left us in an indigo limbo in which we ourselves appeared to float, like clouds, since we could hardly see the ground beneath our feet.

Finally we reached the paving, marking the last climb,

and were out of danger, because we were no longer in the watercourses. We were exhausted, and more or less barefoot. It had taken us three hours to cover this final league.

However, the fine weather returned and the Majorcan steamer was able to renew its weekly trips to Barcelona, Our invalid seemed too weak to be able to undertake the journey, but also too sick to take another week in Majorca. It was a terrible situation; there were days in which I lost all hope and courage. To console us, Maria Antonia and her gossips from the village never tired of repeating to us, in chorus, the most edifying speeches about our future life.

"That consumptive," they said, "will go to hell. Firstly, because he's a consumptive and secondly, because he never confesses."

"If this goes on, when he dies he won't be buried in holy ground, and as no-one will want to dig his grave, his friends will have to do the best they can. You'll see how that turns out. As for me, I want no part in it."

"Nor I!"

"Nor me, Amen!"

Finally, we left, and I have already described our reception on the boat over to Barcelona.

When we arrived in Barcelona, we were so keen to leave behind forever that inhuman race, that we did not have the patience to wait to disembark. I wrote a note to M. Belves, the French naval commander, and sent it to him by boat. Some moments after receiving it, he came to fetch us in his tender, and took us to his ship the *Méleágre*.

Stepping aboard that beautiful man of war, maintained with the cleanliness and elegance of a drawing-room, seeing ourselves surrounded by kind, intelligent faces, receiving the generous and solicitous attention of the captain, the ship's doctor, the officers, and the entire crew; shaking hands with the excellent, and spiritual, French consul, M. Gautier d'Arc, we gave a jump for joy on the bridge, and from the depths of our being emerged a shout:

"*Vive la France!*"

We had the impression of having travelled around the world, and having come back to civilisation, after having abandoned the savages of Polynesia.

Now, the moral of this tale, occasionally puerile, perhaps, but always sincere, is that man is not made to live among trees, surrounded by stones, an open sky, a blue sea, flowers and mountains, but rather among his fellow men.

In the troubled days of youth, we imagine that solitude is a great refuge against all blows, the great remedy for the wounds of combat; this is a grave error, and experience teaches us that, where we cannot live in peace with our fellows, there is no poetic wonder, nor artistic joy, capable of spanning the abyss that opens up in the depths of the soul.

I had always dreamed of living in a desert, and every sincere dreamer will admit to having shared that same fantasy. However, believe me, my friends, our heart is too accustomed to love for us to be able to dispense with the need for others; and the best we can do is to mutually support each other; because we are like children of the same family, we pester each other, fight each other, even hit each other, yet even so, we cannot bring ourselves to abandon each other.

THE END